L I F E
D E A T H
A N D
IMMORTALITY

For more information please call the
Bahai's of Berks County
610-678-0859
1-800-228-6483

L I F E
D E A T H
A N D
IMMORTALITY

THE
JOURNEY
OF
THE
SOUL

Compiled by

TERRILL G. HAYES, BETTY J. FISHER
RICHARD A. HILL, TERRY J. CASSIDAY

Bahá'í Publishing Trust
Wilmette, Illinois

Bahá'í Publishing Trust, Wilmette, Illinois 60091

Copyright © 1994 by the National Spiritual Assembly
of the Bahá'ís of the United States
All Rights Reserved. First edition 1994
Printed in the United States of America
00 99 98   4 3 2

Library of Congress Cataloging-in-Publication Data

Life, death, and immortality : the journey of the soul / compiled by
    Terrill G. Hayes . . . [et al.]. — 1st ed.
            p.   cm.
    Includes bibliographical references.
    ISBN 0-87743-223-6
    1. Spiritual life—Bahai Faith. 2. Future life—Bahai Faith.
    3. Bahai Faith—Doctrines.   I. Hayes, Terrill, G., 1948–
BP380.L54   1994
297'.9323—dc20   94-9189
                                                            CIP

DESIGN BY SHARONE BURRIS

O peoples of the earth! God, the Eternal Truth,
is My witness that streams of fresh and soft-flowing
waters have gushed from the rocks through the sweetness
of the words uttered by your Lord, the Unconstrained;
and still ye slumber. Cast away that which ye possess,
and, on the wings of detachment, soar beyond
all created things. Thus biddeth you the Lord of creation,
the movement of Whose Pen hath revolutionized
the soul of mankind.

Know ye from what heights your Lord,
the All-Glorious, is calling? Think ye that ye have recognized
the Pen wherewith your Lord, the Lord of all names,
commandeth you? Nay, by My life! Did ye but know it,
ye would renounce the world, and would hasten
with your whole hearts to the presence of the Well-Beloved.
Your spirits would be so transported by His Word
as to throw into commotion the Greater World—
how much more this small and petty one!
Thus have the showers of My bounty been poured down
from the heaven of My loving-kindness,
as a token of My grace, that ye may be of the thankful.

—Bahá'u'lláh

CONTENTS

3

THE DAILY STRUGGLE
FREEING THE SOUL'S POTENTIAL

4

ETERNITY
LIFE BEYOND THIS LIFE

5

THIS LIFE AND THE NEXT
DISCOVERIES, ASSOCIATION, AND
COMMUNICATION

6

PRAYERS AND MEDITATIONS FOR SPIRITUAL PROGRESS

APPENDICES

REFERENCES   187

The Bahá'í Faith is an independent world religion with adherents in every country. Its Founder was Mírzá Ḥusayn 'Alí (1817–1892), known as Bahá'u'lláh, the "Glory of God." In 1863 He proclaimed that He was the Promised One of all ages, the fulfillment of thousands of years of religious prophecy. The central principles of His religion are the oneness of God, the oneness of religion, and the oneness of humanity. Bahá'ís believe that religious truth is not absolute but relative; that Divine Revelation is a continuous and progressive process; that all the great religions of the world are divine in origin; and that their missions represent successive stages in the evolution of human society. The Bahá'í writings provide guidance for establishing peace and world order and offer specific guidance that helps Bahá'ís fulfill the basic purpose of human life: to know and to worship God.

FOREWORD

However knowledgeable we may become about the divine origins of our cosmos, however confident we may be about the destiny of humankind on this small planet, we never escape one abiding concern—that each of us will soon pass from this earthly existence. Therefore, whatever guidance and meaning religion can provide to help us conquer the challenges of our daily lives, possibly the greatest comfort it can offer is the assurance that our physical existence has a purpose, that somehow our earthly life, so fleeting and so fragile, is preparing us for something more enduring.

The Bahá'í Faith has a vast amount of information to impart about the reality that awaits us after death. It is a vision that offers consolation, but it also has the power to invigorate our lives here and now because it explains the relevance of our performance in this life to what we will experience in the continuation of our lives beyond physical reality.

For example, the Bahá'í writings explain that our physical experience is unique. We get no second chance, no reincarnation, because we do not need it. Our brief lives, however chaotic and unjust they may sometimes seem to us, are quite adequate to provide us with the spiritual tools we will need to continue our progress in the next world. In fact, this life is important precisely because it does prepare us for the next stage of our existence in the same way that the gestation of the child in the womb prepares it for participation in this life. Yet our spiritual development is not completed in this physical life any more than the birth of an infant signals the completion of its growth. From the Bahá'í view the journey of the soul is a process of endless growth and infinite possibilities. In this respect the Bahá'í belief about the afterlife differs significantly from some other views, which assert that the afterlife is but a reflection of this life, a judgment: we spend eternity in some sort of heaven if we have done well, in a hell if we have not. In contrast, the Bahá'í writings tell us that our lives are never static; even in the next world we will continue changing and developing. For while the human soul will never change its essence—will never become something other than a human soul—it is infinitely perfectible. We are, by nature, always in the process of becoming, and we always will be.

The encouraging part of Bahá'í belief in the eternal progress of the soul is the promise of endless growth and change. The intimidating part of this belief is that we are given only one soul to work with for the rest of eternity. Whether we like ourselves or not, we are stuck with ourselves forever. This belief alone should prompt us to pay careful attention to our progress in this physical life. Since we will be born into the afterlife with the same spiritual condition we have at our body's demise, we would do well to seize every opportunity we have in this life for spiritual development so that our birth may be a felicitous occasion.

The Bahá'í writings also describe some important aspects of the transition to the next stage of our existence. Bahá'u'lláh says that at the point of death, when the soul ceases to associate with the body, we will evaluate our lives: "It is clear and evident that all men shall, after their physical death, estimate the worth of their deeds, and realize all that their hands have wrought." Therefore, He exhorts us to evaluate our lives on a daily basis, to bring ourselves "to account each day" before we are "summoned to a reckoning; for death, unheralded, shall come upon thee and thou shalt be called to give account for thy deeds."[1]

After death, when our souls have ceased to associate with our physical bodies, we will experience emotions appropriate to the progress we have made in our spiritual development. Bahá'-u'lláh tells us that "the followers of the one true God shall, the moment they depart out of this life, experience such joy and gladness as would be impossible to describe, while they that live in error shall be seized with such fear and trembling, and shall be filled with such consternation, as nothing can exceed."[2]

And what happens after our initial experience in the after-life? The Bahá'í writings hint that, among other things, we will meet other souls, continue to learn, and generally participate in the work of the divine world. Yet, exciting and encouraging as this may sound, the Bahá'í writings note that we are permitted to know relatively little about the existence that awaits us. One reason for this concealment is that words are inadequate to

---

1. Bahá'u'lláh, *Gleanings from the Writings of Bahá'u'lláh,* trans. Shoghi Effendi, 1st pocket-size ed. (Wilmette, Ill.: Bahá'í Publishing Trust, 1983), 171; *The Hidden Words,* trans. Shoghi Effendi (Wilmette, Ill: Bahá'í Publishing Trust, 1939), Arabic, no. 31.

2. Bahá'u'lláh, *Gleanings* 171.

portray spiritual reality. Bahá'u'lláh observes: "The nature of the soul after death can never be described, nor is it meet and permissible to reveal its whole character to the eyes of men." He also says that the world beyond "is as different from this world as this world is different from that of the child while still in the womb of its mother."[3]

The most important reason for concealing what awaits us beyond our physical lives is the need for us to focus attention on this life. To know what awaits us might render us incapable of abiding this life, as many of those who have had "near death" experiences seem to confirm. Bahá'u'lláh explains that, if we were shown what awaits the souls of those who at the hour of death are "sanctified from the vain imaginings of the peoples of the world," our "whole being" would "instantly blaze out" in our great longing to attain "that most exalted, that sanctified and resplendent station."[4]

The teachings of the Bahá'í Faith cover many other subjects to help us deal effectively with the daily affairs of our lives—from laws of personal conduct and comportment to the most wide ranging issues of global peace and the governance of our planet. But underlying and giving meaning to every aspect of the Bahá'í teachings is the belief in a spiritual reality. Put simply, at the core of Bahá'í belief are the teachings about the existence and destiny of the human soul, a spiritual essence we can only vaguely understand in this life, because "the soul is a sign of God, a heavenly gem whose reality the most learned of men hath failed

---

3. Bahá'u'lláh, *Gleanings* 156, 157.

4. Bahá'u'lláh, *Gleanings* 156.

to grasp, and whose mystery no mind, however acute, can ever hope to unravel."[5]

Nevertheless, we can know certain properties of the soul, and we can understand certain laws governing its progress. Acquiring such knowledge can have a dramatic effect on how we think about ourselves and how we conduct our lives. For example, the Bahá'í writings state that, while the human soul is an emanation from God, it takes its beginning and identity at conception when the soul associates with the body. Once begun, the soul is eternal; it is not dependent on the existence of the body.

Neither is the soul's progress impaired by infirmities of mind or body. Bahá'u'lláh says, "Know thou that the soul of man is exalted above, and is independent of all infirmities of body or mind."[6] These impairments do not hinder the soul's progress because the soul is not in the body. The soul associates through the body in much the same way as a light becomes apparent in a mirror or as a radio or television signal becomes perceptible through a receiver. If a mirror becomes dirty or shattered, it may not reflect the light, but the light is still resplendent. Likewise, if the television set is in disrepair, we may not be able to see a program, but the signal from the station is not adversely affected.

Since we communicate through physical means in this stage of existence, we may have trouble understanding or communicating with someone whose soul must operate through a dysfunctional body, whether that impairment results from emo-

---

5. Bahá'u'lláh, *Gleanings* 158–59.
6. Bahá'u'lláh, *Gleanings* 153–54.

tional, mental, or physical infirmities. But when the association between the soul and the body ceases at death, the soul is released from this relationship and manifests its true condition. According to Bahá'u'lláh, "every malady afflicting the body of man is an impediment that preventeth the soul from manifesting its inherent might and power. When it leaveth the body, however, it will evince such ascendancy, and reveal such influence as no force on earth can equal."[7]

The association between the soul and the body is extremely important for our spiritual development, but spiritual progress can also take place in other ways when it is not possible in this life. For example, the Bahá'í writings assure us that for those who die prematurely, who are physically or mentally impaired, or who for other reasons are unable to use adequately the physical stage of existence, other means for spiritual development and enlightenment will be provided in the next stage of life.

The reason progress can take place in the afterlife is simple. All the powers that distinguish us as human beings—reason, memory, abstract thought, inventiveness, willpower—are properties of the soul, not the body. Many scientists theorize that the essential capacities of the human reality are nothing more than the powers of a highly evolved brain. The Bahá'í writings assert that all distinctive human powers are functions and faculties of the soul. The brain may channel the soul's will into specific acts, but memory, thought, decisions, willpower, identity itself all derive from the soul.

---

7. Bahá'u'lláh, *Gleanings* 154.

All of the assertions in the Bahá'í writings about the nature and eternal life of the soul may provide us with some degree of solace and encouragement as we go about the business of living our mundane lives, but they also lead us to one unavoidable question. If we are essentially spiritual beings and if our purpose in this life is to prepare for our birth into a purely spiritual reality, why would an all-powerful, all-loving God ordain that we begin our eternal lives in an environment that often seems calculated to prevent, or at least to encumber, spiritual development?

The Bahá'í writings respond that we derive a number of important benefits from the physical stage of our eternal spiritual journey. Physical life is important because the soul takes its beginning here, develops the initial concepts of spirituality here, and initiates the eternal process of spiritual growth here. Physical reality is the first classroom for the foundational growth and development of the soul. It is here that we develop the capacity to recognize our spiritual nature and to exercise the responsibility we have for promoting our own spiritual development. In this context, Bahá'u'lláh assures us that "every man hath been, and will continue to be, able of himself to appreciate the Beauty of God, the Glorified. Had he not been endowed with such a capacity, how could he be called to account for his failure?" Since everyone can recognize spirituality in some form, Bahá'u'lláh asserts that "the faith of no man can be conditioned by any one except himself."[8]

---

8. Bahá'u'lláh, *Gleanings* 143.

Nevertheless, we may well wonder how we could be expected to extract spiritual insights and develop spiritual attributes from our physical experience without some assistance. The Bahá'í writings assure us that all the help we need is provided. In this workshop for the soul, this classroom that is physical reality, perfect Teachers, the Prophets or Manifestations of God, appear periodically in history to bring the wisest guidance for us individually and for each stage in the collective advancement of humankind on our planet.

Yet, perfect Educators that They are, these Teachers do not impose Themselves on us. They exemplify human virtue in Their own conduct. They exhort us to follow Them. They provide us with specific laws to help us use well this opportunity for development. But it is not sufficient that we merely recognize the Prophets or appreciate Their sacrificial lives. If we are to benefit from Their instruction, we are required to demonstrate our recognition through obedience to the laws and guidance that They bring. For Bahá'ís, belief necessitates deeds, because spiritual development is only theoretical until it is demonstrated in action. Belief is not achieved by withdrawing from the world but by actively participating in the crucible of human society. This social aspect of the soul's journey derives from the fact that we are not alone. Each of us is a member of an organic family. Our personal well-being is inseparable from the health of the entire human family. We function much as does a cell in the human body. The cell could hardly afford to think of its own well-being as having much meaning apart from the well-being of the body that it serves. The body provides the cell with a necessary environment, and the self-interest of the cell is inextricably bound up in the body's health. Thus we can hardly attend to our own soul's progress without simultaneously attending to the health of the society in which we live. According to Bahá'u'lláh, that society has now evolved into a global community in which the earth is but one household.

In general, then, the Bahá'í writings teach that physical reality is not a separate or lesser creation, but rather an expression of the spiritual world in concrete terms. It is an artistic or poetic form created for the purpose of human instruction. There is nothing abhorrent or demeaning about physical reality or our appropriate use of it because the physical world is the outward, visible aspect of the eternal creation. The Bahá'í writings say that the "spiritual world is like unto the phenomenal world. They are the exact counterpart of each other. Whatever objects appear in this world of existence are the outer pictures of the world of heaven."[9]

There is much more to say about the Bahá'í teachings on the nature of the soul and its endless journey through the worlds of God. It is, after all, an inexhaustibly fascinating subject that elicits within us the most weighty questions we can pose about our reality as human beings. What are we? What are our origins? What is our destiny individually and collectively? What part do we play in our own spiritual advancement? What effects do our

---

9. 'Abdu'l-Bahá, *The Promulgation of Universal Peace: Talks Delivered by 'Abdu'l-Bahá during His Visit to the United States and Canada in 1912,* comp. Howard MacNutt, 2d ed. (Wilmette, Ill.: Bahá'í Publishing Trust, 1982), 10.

actions in this life have on our experience in the world beyond? How does a loving God care for those who endure suffering, injustice, deprivation, abuse, and disability in this life? How does a just God respond to those who have perpetrated injustice, violence, and the myriad other shameful acts that give pain to others? What is the fate of those who ignore their own spiritual reality? What is the destiny of humankind on this planet? Will we encounter our loved ones in the world beyond? Will we continue to learn? Will we have access to books and learned souls? Will we have goals to achieve, a purpose? Will we have any sort of free will?

The Bahá'í writings help us discover answers to these and other heartfelt questions, answers that can play an important role in helping us face meaningfully a life that sometimes does not seem to make much sense. The answers are never dogmatic. They are sometimes veiled. They always require something of us—the willingness to abandon our preconceptions, the daring to open our hearts and minds, the determination to set aside sufficient time for meditation and prayer, and the resourcefulness to apply rigorously our most subtle faculties of reason, creativity, and imagination.

—JOHN S. HATCHER

LIFE
DEATH
AND
IMMORTALITY

1

DEATH
A
TRANSITION
TO
LIFE

RETURNING TO GOD

Ye, and all ye possess, shall pass away. Ye shall, most certainly, return to God, and shall be called to account for your doings in the presence of Him Who shall gather together the entire creation . . .

Bahá'u'lláh   1

This mortal life is sure to perish; its pleasures are bound to fade away and ere long ye shall return unto God, distressed with pangs of remorse, for presently ye shall be roused from your slumber, and ye shall soon find yourselves in the presence of God and will be asked of your doings.

The Báb   2

All men have proceeded from God and unto Him shall all return. All shall appear before Him for judgment. He is the Lord of the Day of Resurrection, of Regeneration and of Reckoning, and His revealed Word is the Balance.

The Báb   3

This earthly life shall come to an end, and everyone shall expire and return unto my Lord God Who will reward with the choicest gifts the deeds of those who endure with patience. Verily thy God assigneth the measure of all created things as He willeth, by virtue of His behest; and those who conform to the good-pleasure of your Lord, they are indeed among the blissful.

THE BÁB   4

Verily God shall soon reward thee and those who have believed in His signs with an excellent reward from His presence. Assuredly no God is there other than Him, the All-Possessing, the Most Generous. The revelations of His bounty pervade all created things; He is the Merciful, the Compassionate.

THE BÁB   5

God has created all, and all return to God.

'ABDU'L-BAHÁ   6

THE REAL WORLD

Sorrow not if, in these days and on this earthly plane, things contrary to your wishes have been ordained and manifested by God, for days of blissful joy, of heavenly delight, are assuredly in store for you. Worlds, holy and spiritually glorious, will be unveiled to your eyes. You are destined by Him, in this world and hereafter, to partake of their benefits, to share in their joys, and to obtain a portion of their sustaining grace. To each and every one of them you will, no doubt, attain.

BAHÁ'U'LLÁH   7

Grieve thou not over the troubles and hardships of this nether world, nor be thou glad in times of ease and comfort, for both shall pass away. This present life is even as a swelling wave, or a mirage, or drifting shadows. Could ever a distorted image on the desert serve as refreshing waters? No, by the Lord of Lords! Never can reality and the mere semblance of reality be one, and wide is the difference between fancy and fact, between truth and the phantom thereof.

Know thou that the Kingdom[1] is the real world, and this nether place is only its shadow stretching out. A shadow hath no life of its own; its existence is only a fantasy, and nothing more; it is but images reflected in water, and seeming as pictures to the eye.

'ABDU'L-BAHÁ 8

These few brief days shall pass away, this present life shall vanish from our sight; the roses of this world shall be fresh and fair no more, the garden of this earth's triumphs and delights shall droop and fade. The spring season of life shall turn into the autumn of death, the bright joy of palace halls give way to moonless dark within the tomb. And therefore is none of this worth loving at all, and to this the wise will not anchor his heart.

He who hath knowledge and power will rather seek out the glory of heaven, and spiritual distinction, and the life that dieth not. And such a one longeth to approach the sacred Threshold of God; for in the tavern of this swiftly-passing world the man of God will not lie drunken, nor will he even for a moment take his ease, nor stain himself with any fondness for this earthly life.

'ABDU'L-BAHÁ 9

---

1. Of God.

Mortal charm shall fade away, roses shall give way to thorns, and beauty and youth shall live their day and be no more. But that which eternally endureth is the Beauty of the True One, for its splendor perisheth not and its glory lasteth for ever; its charm is all-powerful and its attraction infinite. Well is it then with that countenance that reflecteth the splendor of the Light of the Beloved One!

'ABDU'L-BAHÁ   10

This phenomenal world will not remain in an unchanging condition even for a short while. Second after second it undergoes change and transformation. Every foundation will finally become collapsed; every glory and splendor will at last vanish and disappear, but the Kingdom of God is eternal and the heavenly sovereignty and majesty will stand firm, everlasting. Hence in the estimation of a wise man the mat in the Kingdom of God is preferable to the throne of the government of the world.

'ABDU'L-BAHÁ   11

THE CONTINUITY OF EXISTENCE

That still another life should exist is thus certain, and, just as the vegetable kingdom is unaware of the world of man, so we, too, know not of the Great Life hereafter that followeth the life of man here below. Our noncomprehension of that life, however, is no proof of its nonexistence. The mineral world, for instance, is utterly unaware of the world of man and cannot comprehend it, but the ignorance of a thing is no proof of its nonexistence. Numerous and conclusive proofs exist that go to show that this infinite world cannot end with this human life.

'ABDU'L-BAHÁ 12

According to divine philosophy there are two important and universal conditions in the world of material phenomena: one which concerns life, the other concerning death; one relative to existence, the other nonexistence; one manifest in composition, the other in decomposition. Some define existence as the expression of reality or being and nonexistence as nonbeing, imagining that death is annihilation. This is a mistaken idea, for total annihilation is an impossibility. At most, composition is ever subject to decomposition or disintegration—that is to say, existence implies the grouping of material elements in a form or body, and nonexistence is simply the decomposing of these groupings. This is the law of creation in its endless forms and infinite variety of expression. Certain elements have formed the composite creature man. This composite association of the elements in the form of a human body is, therefore, subject to disintegration, which we call death, but after disintegration the elements themselves persist unchanged. Therefore, total annihilation is an impossibility, and existence can never become nonexistence. This would be equivalent to saying that light can become darkness, which is manifestly untrue and impossible. As existence can never become nonexistence, there is no death for man; nay, rather, man is everlasting and ever-living. The rational proof of this is that the atoms of the material elements are transferable from one form of existence to another, from one degree and kingdom to another, lower or higher. For example, an atom of the soil or dust of earth may traverse the kingdoms from mineral to man by successive incorporations into the bodies of the organisms of those kingdoms. At one time it enters into the formation of the mineral or rock; it is then absorbed by the vegetable kingdom and becomes a constituent of the body and fiber of a tree; again it is appropriated by the animal, and at a still later period is found in the body of man. Throughout these degrees of its traversing the kingdoms from one form of phenomenal being to another, it retains its atomic existence and is never annihilated nor relegated to nonexistence.

Nonexistence, therefore, is an expression applied to change of form, but this transformation can never be rightly considered annihilation, for the elements of composition are ever present and existent as we have seen in the journey of the atom through successive kingdoms, unimpaired; hence, there is no death; life is everlasting. So to speak, when the atom entered into the composition of the tree, it died to the mineral kingdom, and when consumed by the animal, it died to the vegetable kingdom, and so on until its transference or transmutation into the kingdom of man; but throughout its traversing it was subject to transformation and not annihilation. Death, therefore, is applicable to a change or transference from one degree or condition to another. In the mineral realm there was a spirit of existence; in the world of plant life and organisms it reappeared as the vegetative spirit; thence it attained the animal spirit and finally aspired to the human spirit. These are degrees and changes but not obliteration, and this is a rational proof that man is everlasting, ever-living. Therefore, death is only a relative term implying change. For example, we will say that this light before me, having reappeared in another incandescent lamp, has died in the one and lives in the other.[2] This is not death in reality. The perfections of the mineral are translated into the vegetable and from thence into the animal, the virtue always attaining a superlative degree in the upward change. In each kingdom we find the same virtues manifesting themselves more fully, proving that the reality has been transferred from a lower to a higher form and kingdom of being. Therefore, nonexistence is only relative and absolute nonexistence inconceivable. This rose . . . will become disintegrated and its symmetry destroyed, but the elements of its composition remain changeless; nothing affects their elemental integrity. They cannot become nonexistent; they are simply transferred from one state to another.

Through his ignorance man fears death, but the death he shrinks from is imaginary and absolutely unreal; it is only human imagination.

The bestowal and grace of God have quickened the realm of existence with life and being. For existence there is neither change nor transformation; existence is ever existence; it can never be translated into nonexistence. It is gradation; a degree below a higher degree is considered as nonexistence. This dust beneath our feet, as compared with our being, is nonexistent. When the human body crumbles into dust, we can say it has become nonexistent; therefore, its dust in relation to living forms of human being is as nonexistent, but in its own sphere it is

---

2. 'Abdu'l-Bahá was speaking to an audience at "L'Alliance Spiritualiste" in Paris on 9 November 1911.

existent, it has its mineral being. Therefore, it is well proved that absolute nonexistence is impossible; it is only relative.

The purpose is this: that the everlasting bestowal of God vouchsafed to man is never subject to corruption. Inasmuch as He has endowed the phenomenal world with being, it is impossible for that world to become nonbeing, for it is the very genesis of God; it is in the realm of origination; it is a creational and not a subjective world, and the bounty descending upon it is continuous and permanent. Therefore, man, the highest creature of the phenomenal world, is endowed with that continuous bounty bestowed by divine generosity without cessation. For instance, the rays of the sun are continuous, the heat of the sun emanates from it without cessation; no discontinuance of it is conceivable. Even so, the bestowal of God is descending upon the world of humanity, never ceasing, continuous, forever. If we say that the bestowal of existence ceases or falters, it is equivalent to saying that the sun can exist with cessation of its effulgence. Is this possible? Therefore, the effulgences of existence are ever present and continuous.

The conception of annihilation is a factor in human degradation, a cause of human debasement and lowliness, a source of human fear and abjection. It has been conducive to the dispersion and weakening of human thought, whereas the realization of existence and continuity has upraised man to sublimity of ideals, established the foundations of human progress and stimulated the development of heavenly virtues; therefore, it behooves man to abandon thoughts of nonexistence and death, which are absolutely imaginary, and see himself ever-living, everlasting in the divine purpose of his creation. He must turn away from ideas which degrade the human soul so that day by day and hour by hour he may advance upward and higher to spiritual perception of the continuity of the human reality. If he dwells upon the thought of nonexistence, he will become utterly incompetent; with weakened willpower his ambition for progress will be lessened and the acquisition of human virtues will cease.

'ABDU'L-BAHÁ   13

The whole physical creation is perishable. These material bodies are composed of atoms; when these atoms begin to separate decomposition sets in, then comes what we call death. This composition of atoms, which constitutes the body or mortal element of any created being, is temporary. When the power of attraction, which holds these atoms together, is withdrawn, the body, as such, ceases to exist.

With the soul it is different. The soul is not a combination of elements, it is not composed of many atoms, it is of one indivisible substance and therefore eternal. It is entirely out of the order of the physical creation; it is immortal!

Scientific philosophy has demonstrated that a *simple* element ("simple" meaning "not composed") is indestructible, eternal. The soul, not being a composition of elements, is, in character, as a simple element, and therefore cannot cease to exist.

The soul, being of that one indivisible substance, can suffer neither disintegration nor destruction, therefore there is no reason for its coming to an end. All things living show signs of their existence, and it follows that these signs could not of themselves exist if that which they express or to which they testify had no being. A thing which does not exist, can, of course, give no sign of its existence. The manifold signs of the existence of the spirit are for ever before us.

. . . .

A non-existent thing, it is agreed, cannot be seen by signs. In order to write a man must exist—one who does not exist cannot write. Writing is, in itself, a sign of the writer's soul and intelligence. The Sacred Writings (with ever the same Teaching) prove the continuity of the spirit.

Consider the aim of creation: is it possible that all is created to evolve and develop through countless ages with this small goal in view—a few years of a man's life on earth? Is it not unthinkable that this should be the final aim of existence?

The mineral evolves till it is absorbed in the life of the plant, the plant progresses till finally it loses its life in that of the animal; the animal, in its turn, forming part of the food of man, is absorbed into human life.

Thus, man is shown to be the sum of all creation, the superior of all created beings, the goal to which countless ages of existence have progressed.

At the best, man spends four-score years and ten in this world—a short time indeed!

Does a man cease to exist when he leaves the body? If his life comes to an end, then all the previous evolution is useless, all has been for nothing! Can one imagine that Creation has no greater aim than this?

The soul is eternal, immortal.

Materialists say, "Where is the soul? What is it? We cannot see it, neither can we touch it."

This is how we must answer them: However much the

mineral may progress, it cannot comprehend the vegetable world. Now, that lack of comprehension does not prove the nonexistence of the plant!

To however great a degree the plant may have evolved, it is unable to understand the animal world; this ignorance is no proof that the animal does not exist!

The animal, be he never so highly developed, cannot imagine the intelligence of man, neither can he realize the nature of his soul. But, again, this does not prove that man is without intellect, or without soul. It only demonstrates this, that one form of existence is incapable of comprehending a form superior to itself.

This flower may be unconscious of such a being as man, but the fact of its ignorance does not prevent the existence of humanity.

In the same way, if materialists do not believe in the existence of the soul, their unbelief does not prove that there is no such realm as the world of spirit. The very existence of man's intelligence proves his immortality; moreover, darkness proves the presence of light, for without light there would be no shadow. Poverty proves the existence of riches, for, without riches, how could we measure poverty? Ignorance proves that knowledge exists, for without knowledge how could there be ignorance?

Therefore the idea of mortality presupposes the existence of immortality—for if there were no Life Eternal, there would be no way of measuring the life of this world!

If the spirit were not immortal, how could the Manifestations of God endure such terrible trials?

Why did Christ Jesus suffer the fearful death on the cross?

Why did Muḥammad bear persecutions?

Why did the Báb make the supreme sacrifice and why did Bahá'u'lláh pass the years of His life in prison?

Why should all this suffering have been, if not to prove the everlasting life of the spirit?

Christ suffered, He accepted all His trials because of the immortality of His spirit. If a man reflects he will understand the spiritual significance of the law of progress; how all moves from the inferior to the superior degree.

It is only a man without intelligence who, after considering these things, can imagine that the great scheme of creation should suddenly cease to progress, that evolution should come to such an inadequate end!

Materialists who reason in this way, and contend that we are unable to *see* the world of spirit, or to perceive the blessings of God, are surely like the animals who have no understanding; having eyes they see not, ears they have, but do not hear. And this lack of sight and hearing is a proof of nothing but their own inferiority; of whom we read in the Qur'án, "They are men who are blind and deaf to the Spirit." They do not use that great gift of God, the power of the understanding, by which they might see with the eyes of the spirit, hear with spiritual ears and also comprehend with a Divinely enlightened heart.

The inability of the materialistic mind to grasp the idea of the Life Eternal is no proof of the non-existence of that life.

The comprehension of that other life depends on our spiritual birth!

My prayer for you is that your spiritual faculties and aspirations may daily increase, and that you will never allow the

material senses to veil from your eyes the glories of the Heavenly
Illumination.

'ABDU'L-BAHÁ   14

UNDERSTANDING DEATH AS A TRANSITION TO ETERNAL LIFE

A friend asked: "How should one look forward to death?"

'Abdu'l-Bahá answered: "How does one look forward to the
goal of any journey? With hope and with expectation. It is even
so with the end of this earthly journey. In the next world, man will
find himself freed from many of the disabilities under which he
now suffers. Those who have passed on through death, have a
sphere of their own. It is not removed from ours; their work, the
work of the Kingdom, is ours; but it is sanctified from what we
call 'time and place.' Time with us is measured by the sun. Where
there is no more sunrise, and no more sunset, that kind of time
does not exist for man. Those who have ascended have different
attributes from those who are still on earth, yet there is no real
separation."

'ABDU'L-BAHÁ   15

Thou hast written of the severe calamity that hath befallen thee—
the death of thy respected husband. That honorable man hath
been so subjected to the stress and strain of this world that his
greatest wish was for deliverance from it. Such is this mortal
abode: a storehouse of afflictions and suffering. It is ignorance

that binds man to it, for no comfort can be secured by any soul in this world, from monarch down to the most humble commoner. If once this life should offer a man a sweet cup, a hundred bitter ones will follow; such is the condition of this world. The wise man, therefore, doth not attach himself to this mortal life and doth not depend upon it; at some moments, even, he eagerly wisheth for death that he may thereby be freed from these sorrows and afflictions. Thus it is seen that some, under extreme pressure of anguish, have committed suicide.

As to thy husband, rest assured. He will be immersed in the ocean of pardon and forgiveness and will become the recipient of bounty and favor.

'ABDU'L-BAHÁ   16

Be not grieved at the death of thy respected husband. He hath, verily, attained the meeting of his Lord at the seat of Truth in the presence of the potent King. Do not suppose that thou hast lost him. The veil shall be lifted and thou shalt behold his face illumined in the Supreme Concourse. Just as God, the Exalted, hath said, "Him will we surely quicken to a happy life." Supreme importance should be attached, therefore, not to this first creation but rather to the future life.

'ABDU'L-BAHÁ   17

The death of that beloved youth and his separation from you have caused the utmost sorrow and grief; for he winged his flight in the flower of his age and the bloom of his youth to the heavenly nest. But he hath been freed from this sorrow-stricken shelter and hath turned his face toward the everlasting nest of the Kingdom, and, being delivered from a dark and narrow world, hath hastened to the sanctified realm of light; therein lieth the consolation of our hearts.

The inscrutable divine wisdom underlieth such heart-rending occurrences. It is as if a kind gardener transferreth a fresh and tender shrub from a confined place to a wide open area. This transfer is not the cause of the withering, the lessening or the destruction of that shrub; nay, on the contrary, it maketh it to grow and thrive, acquire freshness and delicacy, become green and bear fruit. This hidden secret is well known to the gardener, but those souls who are unaware of this bounty suppose that the gardener, in his anger and wrath, hath uprooted the shrub. Yet to those who are aware, this concealed fact is manifest, and this predestined decree is considered a bounty. Do not feel grieved or disconsolate, therefore, at the ascension of that bird of faithfulness; nay, under all circumstances pray for that youth, supplicating for him forgiveness and the elevation of his station.

I hope that ye will attain the utmost patience, composure and resignation, and I entreat and implore at the Threshold of Oneness, begging for forgiveness and pardon. My hope from the infinite bounties of God is that He may shelter this dove of the garden of faith, and cause him to abide on the branch of the Supreme Concourse,[3] that he may sing in the best of melodies the praise and glorification of the Lord of Names and Attributes.

'ABDU'L-BAHÁ   18

---

3. The company of holy souls of the spiritual world.

Although the loss of a son is indeed heart-breaking and beyond the limits of human endurance, yet one who knoweth and understandeth is assured that the son hath not been lost but, rather, hath stepped from this world into another, and she will find him in the divine realm. That reunion shall be for eternity, while in this world separation is inevitable and bringeth with it a burning grief.

Praise be unto God that thou hast faith, art turning thy face toward the everlasting Kingdom and believest in the existence of a heavenly world. Therefore be thou not disconsolate, do not languish, do not sigh, neither wail nor weep; for agitation and mourning deeply affect his soul in the divine realm.

That beloved child addresseth thee from the hidden world: "O thou kind Mother, thank divine Providence that I have been freed from a small and gloomy cage and, like the birds of the meadows, have soared to the divine world—a world which is spacious, illumined, and ever gay and jubilant. Therefore, lament not, O Mother, and be not grieved; I am not of the lost, nor have I been obliterated and destroyed. I have shaken off the mortal form and have raised my banner in this spiritual world. Following this separation is everlasting companionship. Thou shalt find me in the heaven of the Lord, immersed in an ocean of light."

'ABDU'L-BAHÁ   19

Question.—What is the condition of children who die before attaining the age of discretion or before the appointed time of birth?

Answer.—These infants are under the shadow of the favor of God; and as they have not committed any sin and are not soiled with the impurities of the world of nature, they are the centers of the manifestation of bounty, and the Eye of Compassion will be turned upon them.

'ABDU'L-BAHÁ   20

As to those souls who are born into this life as ethereal and radiant entities and yet, on account of their handicaps and trials, are deprived of great and real advantages, and leave the world without having lived to the full—certainly this is a cause for grieving. This is the reason why the universal Manifestations of God unveil Their countenances to man, and endure every calamity and sore affliction, and lay down Their lives as a ransom; it is to make these very people, the ready ones, the ones who have capacity, to become dawning points of light, and to bestow upon them the life that fadeth never.

'ABDU'L-BAHÁ   21

These human conditions may be likened to the matrix of the mother from which a child is to be born into the spacious outer world. At first the infant finds it very difficult to reconcile itself to its new existence. It cries as if not wishing to be separated from its narrow abode and imagining that life is restricted to that limited space. It is reluctant to leave its home, but nature forces it into this world. Having come into its new conditions, it finds that it has passed from darkness into a sphere of radiance; from gloomy and restricted surroundings it has been transferred to a spacious and delightful environment. Its nourishment was the blood of the mother; now it finds delicious food to enjoy. Its new life is filled with brightness and beauty; it looks with wonder and delight upon the mountains, meadows and fields of green, the rivers and fountains, the wonderful stars; it breathes the life-quickening atmosphere; and then it praises God for its release from the confinement of its former condition and attainment to the freedom of a new realm. This analogy expresses the relation of the temporal world to the life hereafter—the transition of the soul of man from darkness and uncertainty to the light and reality of the eternal Kingdom. At first it is very difficult to welcome death, but after attaining its new condition the soul is grateful, for it has been released from the bondage of the limited to enjoy the liberties of the unlimited. It has been freed from a world of sorrow, grief and trials to live in a world of unending bliss and joy. The phenomenal and physical have been abandoned in order that it may attain the opportunities of the ideal and spiritual. Therefore, the souls of those who have passed away from earth and completed their span of mortal pilgrimage . . . have hastened to a world superior to this. They have soared away from these conditions of darkness and dim vision into the realm of light.

'ABDU'L-BAHÁ   22

MEDITATIONS ON
THE TRANSITION TO LIFE

O SON OF MAN!
Thou art My dominion and My dominion perisheth not; wherefore fearest thou thy perishing? Thou art My light and My light shall never be extinguished; why dost thou dread extinction?

Thou art My glory and My glory fadeth not; thou art My robe and My robe shall never be outworn. Abide then in thy love for Me, that thou mayest find Me in the realm of glory.

BAHÁ'U'LLÁH 23

O SON OF THE SUPREME!
I have made death a messenger of joy to thee. Wherefore dost thou grieve? I made the light to shed on thee its splendor. Why dost thou veil thyself therefrom?

BAHÁ'U'LLÁH 24

O SON OF SPIRIT!
With the joyful tidings of light I hail thee: rejoice! To the court of holiness I summon thee; abide therein that thou mayest live in peace for evermore.

BAHÁ'U'LLÁH 25

2

EARTHBOUND
THE
SEDUCTION
OF HUMAN
PLEASURES,
OPPORTUNITIES
FOR ATTAINING
TRUE
HAPPINESS

THE ILLUSION OF EARTHLY LIFE

The generations that have gone on before you—whither are they fled? And those round whom in life circled the fairest and the loveliest of the land, where now are they? Profit by their example, O people, and be not of them that are gone astray.

Others erelong will lay hands on what ye possess, and enter into your habitations. Incline your ears to My words, and be not numbered among the foolish.

For every one of you his paramount duty is to choose for himself that on which no other may infringe and none usurp from him. Such a thing—and to this the Almighty is My witness—is the love of God, could ye but perceive it.

Build ye for yourselves such houses as the rain and floods can never destroy, which shall protect you from the changes and chances of this life. This is the instruction of Him Whom the world hath wronged and forsaken.

BAHÁ'U'LLÁH 1

Say, I swear by the righteousness of God! Erelong the pomp of the ministers of state and the ascendancy of the rulers shall pass away, the palaces of the potentates shall be laid waste and the imposing buildings of the emperors reduced to dust, but what shall endure is that which We have ordained for you in the Kingdom. It behooveth you, O people, to make the utmost endeavor that your names may be mentioned before the Throne and ye may bring forth that which will immortalize your memories throughout the eternity of God, the Lord of all being.

BAHÁ'U'LLÁH 2

Exultest thou over the treasures thou dost possess, knowing they shall perish? Rejoicest thou in that thou rulest a span of earth, when the whole world . . . is worth as much as the black in the eye of a dead ant? Abandon it unto such as have set their affections upon it, and turn thou unto Him Who is the Desire of the world. Whither are gone the proud and their palaces? Gaze thou into their tombs, that thou mayest profit by this example, inasmuch as We made it a lesson unto every beholder. Were the breezes of Revelation to seize thee, thou wouldst flee the world, and turn unto the Kingdom, and wouldst expend all thou possessest, that thou mayest draw nigh unto this sublime Vision.

BAHÁ'U'LLÁH 3

The world is but a show, vain and empty, a mere nothing, bearing the semblance of reality. Set not your affections upon it. Break not the bond that uniteth you with your Creator, and be not of those that have erred and strayed from His ways. Verily I say, the world is like the vapor in a desert, which the thirsty dreameth to be water and striveth after it with all his might, until when he cometh unto it, he findeth it to be mere illusion.

BAHÁ'U'LLÁH 4

Know ye that by "the world" is meant your unawareness of Him

Who is your Maker, and your absorption in aught else but Him. The "life to come," on the other hand, signifieth the things that give you a safe approach to God, the All-Glorious, the Incomparable. Whatsoever deterreth you, in this Day, from loving God is nothing but the world. Flee it, that ye may be numbered with the blest. Should a man wish to adorn himself with the ornaments of the earth, to wear its apparels, or partake of the benefits it can bestow, no harm can befall him, if he alloweth nothing whatever to intervene between him and God, for God hath ordained every good thing, whether created in the heavens or in the earth, for such of His servants as truly believe in Him.

BAHÁ'U'LLÁH 5

O ye loved ones of God! Know ye that the world is even as a mirage rising over the sands, that the thirsty mistaketh for water. The wine of this world is but a vapor in the desert, its pity and compassion but toil and trouble, the repose it proffereth only weariness and sorrow. Abandon it to those who belong to it, and turn your faces unto the Kingdom of your Lord the All-Merciful, that His grace and bounty may cast their dawning splendors over you, and a heavenly table may be sent down for you, and your Lord may bless you, and shower His riches upon you to gladden your bosoms and fill your hearts with bliss, to attract your minds, and cleanse your souls, and console your eyes.

'ABDU'L-BAHÁ 6

Seize ye, O loved ones of the All-Merciful, the chalice of eternal life proffered by the hand of the bountiful favors of your Lord, the Possessor of the entire creation, then drink ye deep therefrom. I swear by God, it will so enrapture you that ye shall arise to magnify His Name and proclaim His utterances amidst the peoples of the earth and shall conquer the cities of the hearts of men in the name of your Lord, the Almighty, the All-Praised.

Moreover, We announce unto everyone the joyful tidings concerning that which We have revealed in Our Most Holy Book[1]—a Book from above whose horizon the day-star of My commandments shineth upon every observer and every observed one. Hold ye fast unto it and fulfill that which is revealed therein. Indeed better is this for you than whatsoever hath been created in the world, did ye but know it. Beware lest the transitory things of human life withhold you from turning unto God, the True One. Ponder ye in your hearts the world and its conflicts and changes, so that ye may discern its merit and the station of those who have set their hearts upon it and have turned away from that which hath been sent down in Our Preserved Tablet.

BAHÁ'U'LLÁH 7

THE LIFE OF THE SPIRIT
VERSUS MATERIAL LIFE

Wert thou to attain to but a dewdrop of the crystal waters of divine knowledge, thou wouldst readily realize that true life is not the life of the flesh but the life of the spirit. For the life of the flesh is common to both men and animals, whereas the

---

1. The Kitáb-i-Aqdas.

life of the spirit is possessed only by the pure in heart who have quaffed from the ocean of faith and partaken of the fruit of certitude. This life knoweth no death, and this existence is crowned by immortality. Even as it hath been said: "He who is a true believer liveth both in this world and in the world to come." If by "life" be meant this earthly life, it is evident that death must needs overtake it.

BAHÁ'U'LLÁH 8

Life is of two kinds: that of the body and that of the spirit. The life of the body is material life, but the life of the spirit expresses the existence of the Kingdom, which consists in receiving the Spirit of God and becoming vivified by the breath of the Holy Spirit. Although the material life has existence, it is pure nonexistence and absolute death for the holy saints. So man exists, and this stone also exists, but what a difference between the existence of man and that of the stone! Though the stone exists, in relation to the existence of man it is nonexistent.

The meaning of eternal life is the gift of the Holy Spirit, as the flower receives the gift of the season, the air, and the breezes of spring. Consider: this flower had life in the beginning like the life of the mineral; but by the coming of the season of spring, of the bounty of the clouds of the springtime, and of the heat of the glowing sun, it attained to another life of the utmost freshness, delicacy and fragrance. The first life of the flower, in comparison to the second life, is death.

'ABDU'L-BAHÁ 9

Entrance into the Kingdom is through the love of God, through detachment, through holiness and chastity, through truthfulness, purity, steadfastness, faithfulness and the sacrifice of life.

These explanations show that man is immortal and lives eternally. For those who believe in God, who have love of God, and faith, life is excellent—that is, it is eternal; but to those souls who are veiled from God, although they have life, it is dark, and in comparison with the life of believers it is nonexistence.

For example, the eye and the nail are living; but the life of the nail in relation to the life of the eye is nonexistent. This stone and this man both exist; but the stone in relation to the existence of man is nonexistent; it has no being; for when man dies, and his body is destroyed and annihilated, it becomes like stone and earth. Therefore, it is clear that although the mineral exists, in relation to man it is nonexistent.

In the same way, the souls who are veiled from God, although they exist in this world and in the world after death, are, in comparison with the holy existence of the children of the Kingdom of God, nonexisting and separated from God.

'ABDU'L-BAHÁ 10

This world is even as the body of man, and the Kingdom of God is as the spirit of life. See how dark and narrow is the physical world of man's body, and what a prey it is to diseases and ills. On the other hand, how fresh and bright is the realm of the human spirit. Judge thou from this metaphor how the world of the Kingdom hath shone down, and how its laws have been made to work in this nether realm. Although the spirit is hidden from view, still its commandments shine out like rays of light upon the world of the human body. In the same way, although the

Kingdom of heaven is hidden from the sight of this unwitting people, still, to him who seeth with the inner eye, it is plain as day.

Wherefore dwell thou ever in the Kingdom, and be thou oblivious of this world below. Be thou so wholly absorbed in the emanations of the spirit that nothing in the world of man will distract thee.

'ABDU'L-BAHÁ 11

Every soul seeketh an object and cherisheth a desire, and day and night striveth to attain his aim. One craveth riches, another thirsteth for glory and still another yearneth for fame, for art, for prosperity and the like. Yet finally all are doomed to loss and disappointment. One and all they leave behind them all that is theirs and empty-handed hasten to the realm beyond, and all their labors shall be in vain. To dust they shall all return, denuded, depressed, disheartened and in utter despair.

But, praised be the Lord, thou art engaged in that which secureth for thee a gain that shall eternally endure; and that is naught but thine attraction to the Kingdom of God, thy faith, and thy knowledge, the enlightenment of thine heart, and thine earnest endeavor to promote the Divine Teachings.

Verily this gift is imperishable and this wealth is a treasure from on high!

'ABDU'L-BAHÁ 12

Supplicate God that ye may become heavenly hosts, spreading the oneness of the world of humanity, taking in hand the armor of peace and conquering the hearts with the sword of love.

Ye are people of the earth, become ye angels of heaven;[2] ye are from the West, draw ye bounties from the East! Be ye illumined, become ye heavenly, become ye merciful and show kindness to all the people!

'ABDU'L-BAHÁ 13

Array yourselves in the perfection of divine virtues. I hope you may be quickened and vivified by the breaths of the Holy Spirit. Then shall ye indeed become the angels of heaven whom Christ promised would appear in this Day to gather the harvest of divine planting. This is my hope. This is my prayer for you.

'ABDU'L-BAHÁ 14

Ask thou of God that the magnet of His love should draw unto thee the knowledge of Him. Once a soul becometh holy in all things, purified, sanctified, the gates of the knowledge of God will open wide before his eyes.

'ABDU'L-BAHÁ 15

---

2. Bahá'u'lláh explains that angels are "holy beings" who "have sanctified themselves from every human limitation, have become endowed with the attributes of the spiritual, and have been adorned with the noble traits of the blessed" (*The Kitáb-i-Íqán* 79–80). 'Abdu'l-Bahá adds that "angels are blessed beings who have severed all ties to this nether world, have been released from the chains of self and the desires of the flesh, and anchored their hearts to the heavenly realms of the Lord"; they are "revealers of God's abounding grace" and "dawning-points of His spiritual bestowals" (*Selections from the Writings of 'Abdu'l-Bahá* 81).

ATTAINING TRUE PARADISE

W here is Paradise, and where is Hell?" Say: "The one is reunion with Me; the other thine own self. . . ."

BAHÁ'U'LLÁH 16

The purpose of God in creating man hath been, and will ever be, to enable him to know his Creator and to attain His Presence. To this most excellent aim, this supreme objective, all the heavenly Books and the divinely-revealed and weighty Scriptures un-equivocally bear witness. Whoso hath recognized the Day Spring of Divine guidance and entered His holy court hath drawn nigh unto God and attained His Presence, a Presence which is the real Paradise, and of which the loftiest mansions of heaven are but a symbol. . . . Whoso hath failed to recognize Him will have condemned himself to the misery of remoteness, a remoteness which is naught but utter nothingness and the essence of the nethermost fire. Such will be his fate, though to outward seeming he may occupy the earth's loftiest seats and be established upon its most exalted throne.

BAHÁ'U'LLÁH 17

As to Paradise: It is a reality and there can be no doubt about it, and now in this world it is realized through love of Me and My good-pleasure. Whosoever attaineth unto it God will aid him in this world below, and after death He will enable him to gain admittance into Paradise whose vastness is as that of heaven and earth. . . . Likewise apprehend thou the nature of hell-fire and

be of them that truly believe. For every act performed there shall
be a recompense according to the estimate of God, and unto this
the very ordinances and prohibitions prescribed by the Almighty
amply bear witness. For surely if deeds were not rewarded and
yielded no fruit, then the Cause of God . . . would prove futile.
Immeasurably high is He exalted above such blasphemies! However, unto them that are rid of all attachments a deed is, verily, its
own reward.

BAHÁ'U'LLÁH 18

Even as Jesus said: "Ye must be born again."[3] Again He saith:
"Except a man be born of water and of the Spirit, he cannot enter
into the Kingdom of God. That which is born of the flesh is flesh;
and that which is born of the Spirit is spirit."[4] The purport of these
words is that whosoever in every dispensation is born of the Spirit
and is quickened by the breath of the Manifestation of Holiness,
he verily is of those that have attained unto "life" and "resurrection" and have entered into the "paradise" of the love of God. And
whosoever is not of them, is condemned to "death" and "deprivation," to the "fire" of unbelief, and to the "wrath" of God. In all
the scriptures, the books and chronicles, the sentence of death,
of fire, of blindness, of want of understanding and hearing, hath
been pronounced against those whose lips have tasted not the
ethereal cup of true knowledge, and whose hearts have been
deprived of the grace of the holy Spirit in their day.

BAHÁ'U'LLÁH 19

---

3. John 3:7.
4. John 3:5–6.

Tear asunder, in My Name, the veils that have grievously blinded your vision, and, through the power born of your belief in the unity of God, scatter the idols of vain imitation. Enter, then, the holy paradise of the good-pleasure of the All-Merciful. Sanctify your souls from whatsoever is not of God, and taste ye the sweetness of rest within the pale of His vast and mighty Revelation, and beneath the shadow of His supreme and infallible authority.

BAHÁ'U'LLÁH 20

We flung open the gates of Paradise unto all the peoples of the world, and exclaimed: "O all ye created things! Strive to gain admittance into Paradise, since ye have, during all your lives, held fast unto virtuous deeds in order to attain unto it." Surely all men yearn to enter therein, but alas, they are unable to do so by reason of that which their hands have wrought. Shouldst thou, however, gain a true understanding of God in thine heart of hearts, ere He hath manifested Himself, thou wouldst be able to recognize Him, visible and resplendent, when He unveileth Himself before the eyes of all men.

THE BÁB 21

No created thing shall ever attain its paradise unless it appeareth in its highest prescribed degree of perfection. For instance, this crystal representeth the paradise of the stone whereof its substance is composed. Likewise there are various stages in the paradise for the crystal itself . . . So long as it was stone it was worthless, but if it attaineth the excellence of ruby—a potentiality which is latent in it—how much a carat will it be worth? Consider likewise every created thing.

Man's highest station, however, is attained through faith in God in every Dispensation and by acceptance of what hath been revealed by Him, and not through learning; inasmuch as in every nation there are learned men who are versed in divers sciences. Nor is it attainable through wealth; for it is similarly evident that among the various classes in every nation there are those possessed of riches. Likewise are other transitory things.

True knowledge, therefore, is the knowledge of God, and this is none other than the recognition of His Manifestation in each Dispensation. Nor is there any wealth save in poverty in all save God and sanctity from aught else but Him—a state that can be realized only when demonstrated towards Him Who is the Dayspring of His Revelation.

THE BÁB 22

There is no paradise more wondrous for any soul than to be exposed to God's Manifestation in His Day, to hear His verses and believe in them, to attain His presence, which is naught but the presence of God, to sail upon the sea of the heavenly kingdom of His good-pleasure, and to partake of the choice fruits of the paradise of His divine Oneness.

THE BÁB 23

There is no paradise, in the estimation of the believers in the Divine Unity, more exalted than to obey God's commandments, and there is no fire in the eyes of those who have known God and His signs, fiercer than to transgress His laws and to oppress another soul, even to the extent of a mustard seed. On the Day of Resurrection God will, in truth, judge all men, and we all verily plead for His grace.

THE BÁB 24

Know thou that . . . purification is regarded as the most accept-
able means for attaining nearness unto God and as the most
meritorious of all deeds. Thus purge thou thine ear that thou
mayest hear no mention besides God, and purge thine eye that it
may behold naught except God, and thy conscience that it
perceive naught other than God, and thy tongue that it proclaim
nothing but God, and thy hand to write naught but the words of
God, and thy knowledge that it comprehend naught except God,
and thy heart that it entertain no wish save God, and in like
manner purge all thine acts and thy pursuits that thou mayest be
nurtured in the paradise of pure love, and perchance mayest
attain the presence of Him Whom God shall make manifest,
adorned with a purity which He highly cherisheth, and be
sanctified from whosoever hath turned away from Him and doth
not support Him. Thus shalt thou manifest a purity that shall
profit thee.

Know thou that every ear which hearkeneth unto His
Words with true faith shall be immune from the fire. Thus the
believer, through his recognition of Him will appreciate the
transcendent character of His heavenly Words, will whole-
heartedly choose Him over others, and will refuse to incline his
affections towards those who disbelieve in Him. Whatever one
gaineth in the life to come is but the fruit of this faith. Indeed any
man whose eye gazeth upon His Words with true faith well
deserveth Paradise; and one whose conscience beareth witness
unto His Words with true faith shall abide in Paradise and attain
the presence of God; and one whose tongue giveth utterance to
His Words with true faith shall have his abode in Paradise,
wherein he will be seized with ecstasy in praise and glorification

of God, the Ever-Abiding, Whose revelations of glory never end and the reviving breaths of Whose holiness never fail. Every hand which setteth down His Words with true faith shall be filled by God, both in this world and in the next, with things that are highly prized; and every breast which committeth His Words to memory, God shall cause, if it were that of a believer, to be filled with His love; and every heart which cherisheth the love of His Words and manifesteth in itself the signs of true faith when His Name is mentioned, and exemplifieth the words, "their hearts are thrilled with awe at the mention of God,"[5] that heart will become the object of the glances of divine favor and on the Day of Resurrection will be highly praised by God.

THE BÁB 25

Now punishments and rewards are said to be of two kinds: first, the rewards and punishments of this life; second, those of the other world. But the paradise and hell of existence are found in all the worlds of God, whether in this world or in the spiritual heavenly worlds. Gaining these rewards is the gaining of eternal life. That is why Christ said, "Act in such a way that you may find eternal life, and that you may be born of water and the spirit, so that you may enter into the Kingdom."[6]

The rewards of this life are the virtues and perfections which adorn the reality of man. For example, he was dark and becomes luminous; he was ignorant and becomes wise; he was neglectful and becomes vigilant; he was asleep and becomes awakened; he

---

5. Qur'án 8:2.
6. Cf. John 3:5

was dead and becomes living; he was blind and becomes a seer; he was deaf and becomes a hearer; he was earthly and becomes heavenly; he was material and becomes spiritual. Through these rewards he gains spiritual birth and becomes a new creature. He becomes the manifestation of the verse in the Gospel where it is said of the disciples that they "were born, not of blood, nor of the will of the flesh, nor of the will of man, but of God"[7]—that is to say, they were delivered from the animal characteristics and qualities which are the characteristics of human nature, and they became qualified with the divine characteristics, which are the bounty of God. This is the meaning of the second birth. For such people there is no greater torture than being veiled from God, and no more severe punishment than sensual vices, dark qualities, lowness of nature, engrossment in carnal desires. When they are delivered through the light of faith from the darkness of these vices, and become illuminated with the radiance of the sun of reality, and ennobled with all the virtues, they esteem this the greatest reward, and they know it to be the true paradise. In the same way they consider that the spiritual punishment—that is to say, the torture and punishment of existence—is to be subjected to the world of nature; to be veiled from God; to be brutal and ignorant; to fall into carnal lusts; to be absorbed in animal frailties; to be characterized with dark qualities, such as falsehood, tyranny, cruelty, attachment to the affairs of the world, and being immersed in satanic ideas. For them, these are the greatest punishments and tortures.

---

7. John 1:13.

Likewise, the rewards of the other world are the eternal life which is clearly mentioned in all the Holy Books, the divine perfections, the eternal bounties and everlasting felicity. The rewards of the other world are the perfections and the peace obtained in the spiritual worlds after leaving this world, while the rewards of this life are the real luminous perfections which are realized in this world, and which are the cause of eternal life, for they are the very progress of existence. It is like the man who passes from the embryonic world to the state of maturity and becomes the manifestation of these words: "Blessed, therefore, be God, the most excellent of Makers."[8] The rewards of the other world are peace, the spiritual graces, the various spiritual gifts in the Kingdom of God, the gaining of the desires of the heart and the soul, and the meeting of God in the world of eternity. In the same way the punishments of the other world—that is to say, the torments of the other world—consist in being deprived of the special divine blessings and the absolute bounties, and falling into the lowest degrees of existence. He who is deprived of these divine favors, although he continues after death, is considered as dead by the people of truth.

'ABDU'L-BAHÁ 26

As to those that have tasted of the fruit of man's earthly existence, which is the recognition of the one true God, exalted be His glory, their life hereafter is such as We are unable to describe. The knowledge thereof is with God, alone, the Lord of all worlds.

BAHÁ'U'LLÁH 27

---

8. Qur'án 23:14.

BRINGING YOURSELF TO ACCOUNT

Set before thine eyes God's unerring Balance and, as one standing in His Presence, weigh in that Balance thine actions every day, every moment of thy life. Bring thyself to account ere thou art summoned to a reckoning, on the Day when no man shall have strength to stand for fear of God, the Day when the hearts of the heedless ones shall be made to tremble.

BAHÁ'U'LLÁH 28

Ye are all created out of water, and unto dust shall ye return. Reflect upon the end that awaiteth you, and walk not in the ways of the oppressor. Give ear unto the verses of God which He Who is the sacred Lote-Tree reciteth unto you. They are assuredly the infallible balance, established by God, the Lord of this world and the next. Through them the soul of man is caused to wing its flight towards the Dayspring of Revelation, and the heart of every true believer is suffused with light. Such are the laws which God hath enjoined upon you, such His commandments prescribed unto you in His Holy Tablet; obey them with joy and gladness, for this is best for you, did ye but know.

BAHÁ'U'LLÁH 29

We verily behold your actions. If We perceive from them the sweet smelling savor of purity and holiness, We will most certainly bless you. Then will the tongues of the inmates of Paradise utter your praise and magnify your names amidst them who have drawn nigh unto God.

BAHÁ'U'LLÁH 30

MEDITATIONS ON THE SEDUCTION OF HUMAN PLEASURES, OPPORTUNITIES FOR ATTAINING TRUE HAPPINESS

O CHILDREN OF NEGLIGENCE!

Set not your affections on mortal sovereignty and rejoice not therein. Ye are even as the unwary bird that with full confidence warbleth upon the bough; till of a sudden the fowler Death throws it upon the dust, and the melody, the form and the color are gone, leaving not a trace. Wherefore take heed, O bondslaves of desire!

BAHÁ'U'LLÁH 31

O MY SERVANT!

Free thyself from the fetters of this world, and loose thy soul from the prison of self. Seize thy chance, for it will come to thee no more.

BAHÁ'U'LLÁH 32

O MY SERVANT!

Abandon not for that which perisheth an everlasting dominion, and cast not away celestial sovereignty for a worldly desire. This is the river of everlasting life that hath flowed from the well-spring of the pen of the merciful; well is it with them that drink!

BAHÁ'U'LLÁH 33

O SON OF MAN!

The light hath shone on thee from the horizon of the sacred Mount and the spirit of enlightenment hath breathed in the Sinai of thy heart. Wherefore, free thyself from the veils of idle fancies and enter into My court, that thou mayest be fit for everlasting life and worthy to meet Me. Thus may death not come upon thee, neither weariness nor trouble.

BAHÁ'U'LLÁH 34

3

THE
DAILY
STRUGGLE
FREEING
THE SOUL'S
POTENTIAL

THE SOUL—A SIGN OF GOD

Know, verily, that the soul is a sign of God, a heavenly gem whose reality the most learned of men hath failed to grasp, and whose mystery no mind, however acute, can ever hope to unravel. It is the first among all created things to declare the excellence of its Creator, the first to recognize His glory, to cleave to His truth, and to bow down in adoration before Him. If it be faithful to God, it will reflect His light, and will, eventually, return unto Him. If it fail, however, in its allegiance to its Creator, it will become a victim to self and passion, and will, in the end, sink in their depths.

Bahá'u'lláh 1

The human soul is, in its essence, one of the signs of God, a mystery among His mysteries. It is one of the mighty signs of the Almighty, the harbinger that proclaimeth the reality of all the worlds of God. Within it lieth concealed that which the world is now utterly incapable of apprehending. Ponder in thine heart the revelation of the Soul of God that pervadeth all His Laws, and contrast it with that base and appetitive nature that hath rebelled against Him, that forbiddeth men to turn unto the Lord of Names, and impelleth them to walk after their lusts and wickedness. Such a soul hath, in truth, wandered far in the path of error. . . .

Bahá'u'lláh 2

Although the human soul has existed on the earth for prolonged times and ages, yet it is phenomenal. As it is a divine sign, when once it has come into existence, it is eternal. The spirit of man has a beginning, but it has no end; it continues eternally. In the same way the species existing on this earth are phenomenal, for it is established that there was a time when these species did not exist on the surface of the earth. Moreover, the earth has not always existed, but the world of existence has always been, for the universe is not limited to this terrestrial globe. The meaning of this is that, although human souls are phenomenal, they are nevertheless immortal, everlasting and perpetual; for the world of things is the world of imperfection in comparison with that of man, and the world of man is the world of perfection in comparison with that of things. When imperfections reach the station of perfection, they become eternal.[1]

'Abdu'l-Bahá 3

RECOGNIZING YOUR
INNER REALITY

Having created the world and all that liveth and moveth therein, He,[2] through the direct operation of His uncon-

---

1. i.e., in the kingdom of man, where alone the Spirit manifests immortality.
2. God.

strained and sovereign Will, chose to confer upon man the unique distinction and capacity to know Him and to love Him—a capacity that must needs be regarded as the generating impulse and the primary purpose underlying the whole of creation. . . . Upon the inmost reality of each and every created thing He hath shed the light of one of His names, and made it a recipient of the glory of one of His attributes. Upon the reality of man, however, He hath focused the radiance of all of His names and attributes, and made it a mirror of His own Self. Alone of all created things man hath been singled out for so great a favor, so enduring a bounty.

Bahá'u'lláh 4

From among all created things He[3] hath singled out for His special favor the pure, the gem-like reality of man, and invested it with a unique capacity of knowing Him and of reflecting the greatness of His glory. This twofold distinction conferred upon him hath cleansed away from his heart the rust of every vain desire, and made him worthy of the vesture with which his Creator hath deigned to clothe him. It hath served to rescue his soul from the wretchedness of ignorance.

This robe with which the body and soul of man hath been adorned is the very foundation of his well-being and development. Oh, how blessed the day when, aided by the grace and might of the one true God, man will have freed himself from the bondage and corruption of the world and all that is therein, and will have attained unto true and abiding rest beneath the shadow of the Tree of Knowledge!

Bahá'u'lláh 5

---

3. God.

Man is the highest species because he is the possessor of the perfections of all the classes—that is, he has a body which grows and which feels. As well as having the perfections of the mineral, of the vegetable and of the animal, he also possesses an especial excellence which the other beings are without—that is, the intellectual perfections. Therefore, man is the most noble of beings.

Man is in the highest degree of materiality, and at the beginning of spirituality—that is to say, he is the end of imperfection and the beginning of perfection. He is at the last degree of darkness, and at the beginning of light; that is why it has been said that the condition of man is the end of the night and the beginning of day, meaning that he is the sum of all the degrees of imperfection, and that he possesses the degrees of perfection. He has the animal side as well as the angelic side, and the aim of an educator is to so train human souls that their angelic aspect may overcome their animal side. Then if the divine power in man, which is his essential perfection, overcomes the satanic power, which is absolute imperfection, he becomes the most excellent among the creatures; but if the satanic power overcomes the divine power, he becomes the lowest of the creatures. That is why he is the end of imperfection and the beginning of perfection. Not in any other of the species in the world of existence is there such a difference, contrast, contradiction and opposition as in the species of man. Thus the reflection of the Divine Light was in man, as in Christ, and see how loved and honored He is! At the same time we see man worshiping a stone, a clod of earth or a tree. How vile he is, in that his object of worship should be the lowest existence—that is, a stone or clay, without spirit; a mountain, a forest or a tree. What shame is greater for man than to worship the lowest existences? In the same way, knowledge is a quality of man, and so is ignorance; truthfulness is a quality of man; so is falsehood; trustworthiness and treachery, justice and injustice, are qualities of man, and so forth. Briefly, all the perfections and virtues, and all the vices, are qualities of man.

Consider equally the differences between individual men. The Christ was in the form of man, and Caiaphas was in the form of man; Moses and Pharaoh, Abel and Cain, Bahá'u'lláh and Yahyá,[4] were men.

Man is said to be the greatest representative of God, and he is the Book of Creation because all the mysteries of beings exist in him. If he comes under the shadow of the True Educator and is rightly trained, he becomes the essence of essences, the light of lights, the spirit of spirits; he becomes the center of the divine appearances, the source of spiritual qualities, the rising-place of heavenly lights, and the receptacle of divine inspirations. If he is deprived of this education, he becomes the manifestation of satanic qualities, the sum of animal vices, and the source of all dark conditions.

The reason of the mission of the Prophets is to educate men, so that this piece of coal may become a diamond, and this fruitless tree may be engrafted and yield the sweetest, most delicious fruits. When man reaches the noblest state in the world of humanity, then he can make further progress in the conditions of perfection, but not in state; for such states are limited, but the divine perfections are endless.

---

4. Mírzá Yahyá Ṣubḥ-i-Azal, half-brother of Bahá'u'lláh, and His irreconcilable enemy.

Both before and after putting off this material form, there is progress in perfection but not in state. So beings are consummated in perfect man. There is no other being higher than a perfect man. But man when he has reached this state can still make progress in perfections but not in state because there is no state higher than that of a perfect man to which he can transfer himself. He only progresses in the state of humanity, for the human perfections are infinite. Thus, however learned a man may be, we can imagine one more learned.

Hence, as the perfections of humanity are endless, man can also make progress in perfections after leaving this world.

'ABDU'L-BAHÁ 6

The superiority of man over the rest of the created world is seen . . . in this, that man has a soul in which dwells the divine spirit; the souls of the lower creatures are inferior in their essence.

There is no doubt then, that of all created beings man is the nearest to the nature of God, and therefore receives a greater gift of the Divine Bounty.

The mineral kingdom possesses the power of existing. The plant has the power of existing and growing. The animal, in addition to existence and growth, has the capacity of moving about, and the use of the faculties of the senses. In the human kingdom we find all the attributes of the lower worlds, with much more added thereto. Man is the sum of every previous creation, for he contains them all.

To man is given the special gift of the intellect by which he is able to receive a larger share of the light Divine. The Perfect Man

is as a polished mirror reflecting the Sun of Truth, manifesting
the attributes of God.

'Abdu'l-Bahá 7

The reality of man is his thought, not his material body. The
thought force and the animal force are partners. Although man is
part of the animal creation, he possesses a power of thought
superior to all other created beings.

'Abdu'l-Bahá 8

It is manifest that beyond this material body, man is endowed
with another reality, which is the world of exemplars constituting
the heavenly body of man. In speaking, man says, "I saw," "I
spoke," "I went." *Who is this I?* It is obvious that this *I* is different
from this body. It is clear that when man is thinking, it is as
though he were consulting with some other person. With whom
is he consulting? It is evident that it is another reality, or one aside
from this body, with whom he enters into consultation when he
thinks, "Shall I do this work or not?" "What will be the result of
my doing this?" Or when he questions the other reality, "What is
the objection to this work if I do it?" And then that reality in man
communicates its opinion to him concerning the point at issue.
Therefore, that reality in man is clearly and obviously other than
his body—an ego with which man enters into consultation and
whose opinion man seeks.

Often a man makes up his mind positively about a matter;
for instance, he determines to undertake a journey. Then he
thinks it over—that is, he consults his inner reality—and finally
concludes that he will give up his journey. What has happened?

Why did he abandon his original purpose? It is evident that he has consulted his inner reality, which expresses to him the disadvantages of such a journey; therefore, he defers to that reality and changes his original intention.

Furthermore, man sees in the world of dreams. He travels in the East; he travels in the West; although his body is stationary, his body is here. It is that reality in him which makes the journey while the body sleeps. There is no doubt that a reality exists other than the outward, physical reality. Again, for instance, a person is dead, is buried in the ground. Afterward, you see him in the world of dreams and speak with him, although his body is interred in the earth. Who is the person you see in your dreams, talk to and who also speaks with you? This again proves that there is another reality different from the physical one which dies and is buried. Thus it is certain that in man there is a reality which is not the physical body. Sometimes the body becomes weak, but that other reality is in its own normal state. The body goes to sleep, becomes as one dead; but that reality is moving about, comprehending things, expressing them and is even conscious of itself.

This other and inner reality is called the heavenly body, the ethereal form which corresponds to this body. This is the conscious reality which discovers the inner meaning of things, for the outer body of man does not discover anything. The inner ethereal reality grasps the mysteries of existence, discovers scientific truths and indicates their technical application. It discovers electricity, produces the telegraph, the telephone and opens the door to the world of arts. If the outer material body did this, the animal would, likewise, be able to make scientific and wonderful discoveries, for the animal shares with man all physical powers and limitations. What, then, is that power which penetrates the realities of existence and which is not to be found in the animal? It is the inner reality which comprehends things, throws light upon the mysteries of life and being, discovers the heavenly Kingdom, unseals the mysteries of God and differentiates man from the brute. Of this there can be no doubt.

'ABDU'L-BAHÁ 9

Man—the true man—is soul, not body; though physically man belongs to the animal kingdom, yet his soul lifts him above the rest of creation. Behold how the light of the sun illuminates the world of matter: even so doth the Divine Light shed its rays in the kingdom of the soul. The soul it is which makes the human creature a celestial entity!

By the power of the Holy Spirit, working through his soul, man is able to perceive the Divine reality of things. All great works of art and science are witnesses to this power of the Spirit.

The same Spirit gives Eternal Life.

'ABDU'L-BAHÁ 10

A man should pause and reflect and be just: his Lord, out of measureless grace, has made him a human being and honored him with the words: "Verily, We created man in the goodliest of forms"[5]—and caused His mercy which rises out of the dawn of oneness to shine down upon him, until he became the wellspring of the words of God and the place where the mysteries of heaven

---

5. Qur'án 95:4.

alighted, and on the morning of creation he was covered with the rays of the qualities of perfection and the graces of holiness.

'Abdu'l-Bahá 11

UNDERSTANDING THE HUMAN SOUL AND SPIRIT

The human soul is exalted above all egress and regress. It is still, and yet it soareth; it moveth, and yet it is still. It is, in itself, a testimony that beareth witness to the existence of a world that is contingent, as well as to the reality of a world that hath neither beginning nor end. Behold how the dream thou hast dreamed is, after the lapse of many years, re-enacted before thine eyes. Consider how strange is the mystery of the world that appeareth to thee in thy dream. Ponder in thine heart upon the unsearchable wisdom of God, and meditate on its manifold revelations. . . .

Bahá'u'lláh 12

Consider the rational faculty with which God hath endowed the essence of man. Examine thine own self, and behold how thy motion and stillness, thy will and purpose, thy sight and hearing, thy sense of smell and power of speech, and whatever else is related to, or transcendeth, thy physical senses or spiritual perceptions, all proceed from, and owe their existence to, this same faculty. So closely are they related unto it, that if in less than the twinkling of an eye its relationship to the human body be severed, each and every one of these senses will cease immediately to exercise its function, and will be deprived of the power to manifest the evidences of its activity. It is indubitably clear and evident that each of these afore-mentioned instruments has depended, and will ever continue to depend, for its proper functioning on this rational faculty, which should be regarded as a sign of the revelation of Him Who is the sovereign Lord of all. Through its manifestation all these names and attributes have been revealed, and by the suspension of its action they are all destroyed and perish.

It would be wholly untrue to maintain that this faculty is the same as the power of vision, inasmuch as the power of vision is derived from it and acteth in dependence upon it. It would, likewise, be idle to contend that this faculty can be identified with the sense of hearing, as the sense of hearing receiveth from the rational faculty the requisite energy for performing its functions.

This same relationship bindeth this faculty with whatsoever hath been the recipient of these names and attributes within the human temple. These diverse names and revealed attributes have been generated through the agency of this sign of God. Immeasurably exalted is this sign, in its essence and reality, above all such names and attributes. Nay, all else besides it will, when compared with its glory, fade into utter nothingness and become a thing forgotten.

BAHÁ'U'LLÁH 13

Question.—What is the difference between the mind, spirit and soul?

Answer.—It has been before explained that spirit is universally divided into five categories: the vegetable spirit, the animal spirit, the human spirit, the spirit of faith, and the Holy Spirit.

The vegetable spirit is the power of growth which is brought about in the seed through the influence of other existences.

The animal spirit is the power of all the senses, which is realized from the composition and mingling of elements; when this composition decomposes, the power also perishes and becomes annihilated. It may be likened to this lamp: when the oil, wick and fire are combined, it is lighted; and when this combination is dissolved—that is to say, when the combined parts are separated from one another—the lamp also is extinguished.

The human spirit which distinguishes man from the animal is the rational soul, and these two names—the human spirit and the rational soul—designate one thing.[6] This spirit, which in the terminology of the philosophers is the rational soul, embraces all beings, and as far as human ability permits discovers the realities of things and becomes cognizant of their peculiarities and effects, and of the qualities and properties of beings. But the human spirit, unless assisted by the spirit of faith, does not become acquainted with the divine secrets and the heavenly realities. It is

---

6. Shoghi Effendi has explained that, "When studying at present, in English, the available Bahá'í writings on the subject of body, soul and spirit, one is handicapped by a certain lack of clarity because not all were translated by the same person, and also there are, as you know, still many Bahá'í writings untranslated. But there is no doubt that spirit and soul seem to have been interchanged in meaning sometimes; soul and mind have, likewise, been interchanged in meaning, no doubt due to difficulties arising from different translations. What the Bahá'ís do believe though is that we have three aspects of our humanness, so to speak, a body, a mind and an immortal identity—soul or spirit. We believe the mind forms a link between the soul and the body, and the two interact on each other" (*Arohanui: Letters from Shoghi Effendi to New Zealand* [Suva, Fiji: Bahá'í Publishing Trust, 1982] 89).

like a mirror which, although clear, polished and brilliant, is still in need of light. Until a ray of the sun reflects upon it, it cannot discover the heavenly secrets.

But the mind is the power of the human spirit. Spirit is the lamp; mind is the light which shines from the lamp. Spirit is the tree, and the mind is the fruit. Mind is the perfection of the spirit and is its essential quality, as the sun's rays are the essential necessity of the sun.

'ABDU'L-BAHÁ 14

The power and the comprehension of the human spirit are of two kinds—that is to say, they perceive and act in two different modes. One way is through instruments and organs: thus with this eye it sees; with this ear it hears; with this tongue it talks. Such is the action of the spirit, and the perception of the reality of man, by means of organs—that is to say, that the spirit is the seer, through the eyes; the spirit is the hearer, through the ear; the spirit is the speaker, through the tongue.

The other manifestation of the powers and actions of the spirit is without instruments and organs. For example, in the state of sleep without eyes it sees; without an ear it hears; without a tongue it speaks; without feet it runs. Briefly, these actions are beyond the means of instruments and organs. How often it happens that it sees a dream in the world of sleep, and its signification becomes apparent two years afterward in corresponding events. In the same way, how many times it happens that a question which one cannot solve in the world of wakefulness is solved in the world of dreams. In wakefulness the eye sees only for a short distance, but in dreams he who is in the East sees the West. Awake he sees the present; in sleep he sees the future. In wakefulness, by means of rapid transit, at the most he can travel only twenty farsakhs[7] an hour; in sleep, in the twinkling of an eye, he traverses the East and West. For the spirit travels in two different ways: without means, which is spiritual traveling; and with means, which is material traveling: as birds which fly, and those which are carried.

In the time of sleep this body is as though dead; it does not see nor hear; it does not feel; it has no consciousness, no perception—that is to say, the powers of man have become inactive, but the spirit lives and subsists. Nay, its penetration is increased, its flight is higher, and its intelligence is greater. To consider that after the death of the body the spirit perishes is like imagining that a bird in a cage will be destroyed if the cage is broken, though the bird has nothing to fear from the destruction of the cage. Our body is like the cage, and the spirit is like the bird. We see that without the cage this bird flies in the world of sleep; therefore, if the cage becomes broken, the bird will continue and exist. Its feelings will be even more powerful, its perceptions greater, and its happiness increased. In truth, from hell it reaches a paradise of delights because for the thankful birds there is no paradise greater than freedom from the cage. That is why with utmost joy and happiness the martyrs hasten to the plain of sacrifice.

In wakefulness the eye of man sees at the utmost as far as one hour of distance[8] because through the instrumentality of the

---

7. One *farsakh* is equivalent to about four miles.
8. It is a Persian custom to reckon distance by time.

body the power of the spirit is thus determined; but with the inner sight and the mental eye it sees America, and it can perceive that which is there, and discover the conditions of things and organize affairs. If, then, the spirit were the same as the body, it would be necessary that the power of the inner sight should also be in the same proportion. Therefore, it is evident that this spirit is different from the body, and that the bird is different from the cage, and that the power and penetration of the spirit is stronger without the intermediary of the body. Now, if the instrument is abandoned, the possessor of the instrument continues to act. For example, if the pen is abandoned or broken, the writer remains living and present; if a house is ruined, the owner is alive and existing. This is one of the logical evidences for the immortality of the soul.

There is another: this body becomes weak or heavy or sick, or it finds health; it becomes tired or rested; sometimes the hand or leg is amputated, or its physical power is crippled; it becomes blind or deaf or dumb; its limbs may become paralyzed; briefly, the body may have all the imperfections. Nevertheless, the spirit in its original state, in its own spiritual perception, will be eternal and perpetual; it neither finds any imperfection, nor will it become crippled. But when the body is wholly subjected to disease and misfortune, it is deprived of the bounty of the spirit, like a mirror which, when it becomes broken or dirty or dusty, cannot reflect the rays of the sun nor any longer show its bounties.

We have already explained that the spirit of man is not in the body because it is freed and sanctified from entrance and exit, which are bodily conditions. The connection of the spirit with the body is like that of the sun with the mirror. Briefly, the human spirit is in one condition. It neither becomes ill from the diseases of the body nor cured by its health; it does not become sick, nor weak, nor miserable, nor poor, nor light, nor small— that is to say, it will not be injured because of the infirmities of the body, and no effect will be visible even if the body becomes weak, or if the hands and feet and tongue be cut off, or if it loses the power of hearing or sight. Therefore, it is evident and certain that the spirit is different from the body, and that its duration is independent of that of the body; on the contrary, the spirit with the utmost greatness rules in the world of the body; and its power and influence, like the bounty of the sun in the mirror, are apparent and visible. But when the mirror becomes dusty or breaks, it will cease to reflect the rays of the sun.

'ABDU'L-BAHÁ 15

Spirit cannot be perceived by the material senses of the physical body, excepting as it is expressed in outward signs and works. The human body is visible, the soul is invisible. It is the soul nevertheless that directs a man's faculties, that governs his humanity.

The soul has two main faculties. (a) As outer circumstances are communicated to the soul by the eyes, ears, and brain of a man, so does the soul communicate its desires and purposes through the brain to the hands and tongue of the physical body, thereby expressing itself. The spirit in the soul is the very essence of life. (b) The second faculty of the soul expresses itself in the world of vision, where the soul inhabited by the spirit has its being, and functions without the help of the material bodily senses. There, in the realm of vision, the soul sees without the help of the physical eye, hears without the aid of the physical ear, and travels without dependence upon physical motion. It is, therefore, clear that the spirit in the soul of man can function through the physical body by using the organs of the ordinary senses, and that it is able also to live and act without their aid in the world of vision. This proves without a doubt the superiority of the soul of man over his body, the superiority of spirit over matter.

For example, look at this lamp: is not the light within it superior to the lamp which holds it? However beautiful the form of the lamp may be, if the light is not there its purpose is unfulfilled, it is without life—a dead thing. The lamp needs the light, but the light does not need the lamp.

The spirit does not need a body, but the body needs spirit, or it cannot live. The soul can live without a body, but the body without a soul dies.

If a man lose his sight, his hearing, his hand or his foot, should his soul still inhabit the body he lives, and is able to manifest divine virtues. On the other hand, without the spirit it would be impossible for a perfect body to exist.

'Abdu'l-Bahá 16

There are in the world of humanity three degrees; those of the body, the soul, and spirit.

The body is the physical or animal degree of man. From the bodily point of view man is a sharer of the animal kingdom. The bodies alike of men and animals are composed of elements held together by the law of attraction.

Like the animal, man possesses the faculties of the senses, is subject to heat, cold, hunger, thirst, etc.; unlike the animal, man has a rational soul, the human intelligence.

This intelligence of man is the intermediary between his body and his spirit.

When man allows the spirit, through his soul, to enlighten his understanding, then does he contain all Creation; because man, being the culmination of all that went before and thus superior to all previous evolutions, contains all the lower world within himself. Illumined by the spirit through the instrumentality of the soul, man's radiant intelligence makes him the crowning-point of Creation.

But on the other hand, when man does not open his mind and heart to the blessing of the spirit, but turns his soul towards the material side, towards the bodily part of his nature, then is he fallen from his high place and he becomes inferior to the inhabitants of the lower animal kingdom. In this case the man is in a sorry plight! For if the spiritual qualities of the soul, open to the breath of the Divine Spirit, are never used, they become atrophied, enfeebled, and at last incapable; whilst the soul's material qualities alone being exercised, they become terribly powerful— and the unhappy, misguided man, becomes more savage, more unjust, more vile, more cruel, more malevolent than the lower animals themselves. All his aspirations and desires being strengthened by the lower side of the soul's nature, he becomes more and more brutal, until his whole being is in no way superior to that of the beasts that perish. Men such as this plan to work evil, to hurt and to destroy; they are entirely without the spirit of Divine compassion, for the celestial quality of the soul has been dominated by that of the material. If, on the contrary, the spiritual nature of the soul has been so strengthened that it holds the material side in subjection, then does the man approach the Divine; his humanity becomes so glorified that the virtues of the Celestial Assembly are manifested in him; he radiates the Mercy of God, he stimulates the spiritual progress of mankind, for he becomes a lamp to show light on their path.

You perceive how the soul is the intermediary between the body and the spirit. In like manner is this tree[9] the intermediary between the seed and the fruit. When the fruit of the tree appears and becomes ripe, then we know that the tree is perfect; if the tree bore no fruit it would be merely a useless growth, serving no purpose!

When a soul has in it the life of the spirit, then does it bring forth good fruit and become a Divine tree. I wish you to try to understand this example. I hope that the unspeakable goodness of God will so strengthen you that the celestial quality of your soul, which relates it to the spirit, will for ever dominate the material side, so entirely ruling the senses that your soul will approach the perfections of the Heavenly Kingdom. May your faces, being steadfastly set towards the Divine Light, become so luminous that all your thoughts, words and actions will shine with the Spiritual Radiance dominating your souls, so that in the gatherings of the world you will show perfection in your life.

Some men's lives are solely occupied with the things of this world; their minds are so circumscribed by exterior manners

---

9. A small orange-tree on the table nearby.

and traditional interests that they are blind to any other realm of existence, to the spiritual significance of all things! They think and dream of earthly fame, of material progress. Sensuous delights and comfortable surroundings bound their horizon, their highest ambitions center in successes of worldly conditions and circumstances! They curb not their lower propensities; they eat, drink, and sleep! Like the animal, they have no thought beyond their own physical well-being. It is true that these necessities must be despatched. Life is a load which must be carried on while we are on earth, but the cares of the lower things of life should not be allowed to monopolize all the thoughts and aspirations of a human being. The heart's ambitions should ascend to a more glorious goal, mental activity should rise to higher levels! Men should hold in their souls the vision of celestial perfection, and there prepare a dwelling-place for the inexhaustible bounty of the Divine Spirit.

Let your ambition be the achievement on earth of a Heavenly civilization! I ask for you the supreme blessing, that you may be so filled with the vitality of the Heavenly Spirit that you may be the cause of life to the world.

'ABDU'L-BAHÁ 17

DEVELOPING YOUR SOUL

And now, concerning thy question regarding the creation of man. Know thou that all men have been created in the nature made by God, the Guardian, the Self-Subsisting. Unto each one hath been prescribed a pre-ordained measure, as decreed in God's mighty and guarded Tablets. All that which ye potentially possess can, however, be manifested only as a result of your own volition. Your own acts testify to this truth.

BAHÁ'U'LLÁH 18

Every soul is fashioned after the nature of God, each being pure and holy at his birth. Afterwards, however, the individuals will vary according to what they acquire of virtues or vices in this world. Although all existent beings are in their very nature created in ranks or degrees, for capacities are various, nevertheless every individual is born holy and pure. . . .

'ABDU'L-BAHÁ 19

In the beginning of his human life man was embryonic in the world of the matrix. There he received capacity and endowment for the reality of human existence. The forces and powers necessary for this world were bestowed upon him in that limited condition. In this world he needed eyes; he received them potentially in the other. He needed ears; he obtained them there in readiness and preparation for his new existence. The powers requisite in this world were conferred upon him in the world of the matrix so that when he entered this realm of real existence he not only possessed all necessary functions and powers but found provision for his material sustenance awaiting him.

Therefore, in this world he must prepare himself for the life beyond. That which he needs in the world of the Kingdom must be obtained here. Just as he prepared himself in the world of the matrix by acquiring forces necessary in this sphere of existence, so, likewise, the indispensable forces of the divine existence must be potentially attained in this world.

'Abdu'l-Bahá 20

What is he[10] in need of in the Kingdom which transcends the life and limitation of this mortal sphere? That world beyond is a world of sanctity and radiance; therefore, it is necessary that in this world he should acquire these divine attributes. In that world there is need of spirituality, faith, assurance, the knowledge and love of God. These he must attain in this world so that after his ascension from the earthly to the heavenly Kingdom he shall find all that is needful in that eternal life ready for him.

That divine world is manifestly a world of lights; therefore, man has need of illumination here. That is a world of love; the love of God is essential. It is a world of perfections; virtues, or perfections, must be acquired. That world is vivified by the breaths of the Holy Spirit; in this world we must seek them. That is the Kingdom of everlasting life; it must be attained during this vanishing existence.

By what means can man acquire these things? How shall he obtain these merciful gifts and powers? First, through the knowledge of God. Second, through the love of God. Third, through faith. Fourth, through philanthropic deeds. Fifth, through self-sacrifice. Sixth, through severance from this world. Seventh, through sanctity and holiness. Unless he acquires these forces

---

10. A human being.

and attains to these requirements, he will surely be deprived of the life that is eternal. But if he possesses the knowledge of God, becomes ignited through the fire of the love of God, witnesses the great and mighty signs of the Kingdom, becomes the cause of love among mankind and lives in the utmost state of sanctity and holiness, he shall surely attain to second birth, be baptized by the Holy Spirit and enjoy everlasting existence.

Is it not astonishing that although man has been created for the knowledge and love of God, for the virtues of the human world, for spirituality, heavenly illumination and eternal life, nevertheless, he continues ignorant and negligent of all this? Consider how he seeks knowledge of everything except knowledge of God. For instance, his utmost desire is to penetrate the mysteries of the lowest strata of the earth. Day by day he strives to know what can be found ten meters below the surface, what he can discover within the stone, what he can learn by archaeological research in the dust. He puts forth arduous labors to fathom terrestrial mysteries but is not at all concerned about knowing the mysteries of the Kingdom, traversing the illimitable fields of the eternal world, becoming informed of the divine realities, discovering the secrets of God, attaining the knowledge of God, witnessing the splendors of the Sun of Truth and realizing the glories of everlasting life. He is unmindful and thoughtless of these. How much he is attracted to the mysteries of matter, and how completely unaware he is of the mysteries of Divinity! Nay, he is utterly negligent and oblivious of the secrets of Divinity. How great his ignorance! How conducive to his degradation! It is as if a kind and loving father had provided a library of wonderful books for his son in order that he might be informed of the mysteries of creation, at the same time surrounding him with every means of comfort and enjoyment, but the son amuses himself with pebbles and playthings, neglectful of all his father's gifts and provision. How ignorant and heedless is man! The Father has willed for him eternal glory, and he is content with blindness and deprivation. The Father has built for him a royal palace, but he is playing with the dust; prepared for him garments of silk, but he prefers to remain unclothed; provided for him delicious foods and fruits, while he seeks sustenance in the grasses of the field.

'ABDU'L-BAHÁ 21

The material world is the world of corruption and death. It is the world of evil and darkness, of animalism and ferocity, bloodthirstiness, ambition and avarice, of self-worship, egotism and passion; it is the world of nature. Man must strip himself of all these imperfections, must sacrifice these tendencies which are peculiar to the outer and material world of existence.

On the other hand, man must acquire heavenly qualities and attain divine attributes. He must become the image and likeness of God. He must seek the bounty of the eternal, become the manifestor of the love of God, the light of guidance, the tree of life and the depository of the bounties of God. That is to say, man must sacrifice the qualities and attributes of the world of nature for the qualities and attributes of the world of God. For instance, consider the substance we call iron. Observe its qualities; it is solid, black, cold. These are the characteristics of iron. When the same iron absorbs heat from the fire, it sacrifices its attribute of solidity for the attribute of fluidity. It sacrifices its attribute of darkness for the attribute of light, which is a quality of the fire. It sacrifices its attribute of coldness to the quality of heat which the fire possesses so that in the iron there remains no solidity, darkness or cold. It becomes illumined and transformed, having sacrificed its qualities to the qualities and attributes of the fire.

Likewise, man, when separated and severed from the attributes of the world of nature, sacrifices the qualities and exigencies of that mortal realm and manifests the perfections of the Kingdom, just as the qualities of the iron disappeared and the qualities of the fire appeared in their place.

Every man trained through the teachings of God and illumined by the light of His guidance, who becomes a believer in God and His signs and is enkindled with the fire of the love of God, sacrifices the imperfections of nature for the sake of divine perfections. . . . May the divine light become manifest upon your faces, the fragrances of holiness refresh your nostrils and the breath of the Holy Spirit quicken you with eternal life.

'Abdu'l-Bahá 22

The retina of outer vision, though sensitive and delicate, may, nevertheless, be a hindrance to the inner eye which alone can perceive. The bestowals of God which are manifest in all phenomenal life are sometimes hidden by intervening veils of mental and mortal vision which render man spiritually blind and incapable, but when those scales are removed and the veils rent asunder, then the great signs of God will become visible, and he will witness the eternal light filling the world. The bestowals of God are all and always manifest. The promises of heaven are ever present. The favors of God are all-surrounding, but should the conscious eye of the soul of man remain veiled and darkened, he will be led to deny these universal signs and remain deprived of these manifestations of divine bounty. Therefore, we must endeavor with heart and soul in order that the veil covering the eye of inner vision may be removed, that we may behold the manifestations of the signs of God, discern His mysterious graces and realize that material blessings as compared with spiritual bounties are as nothing. The spiritual blessings of God are greatest. When we were in the mineral kingdom, although we were endowed with certain gifts and powers, they were not to be compared with the blessings of the human kingdom. In the matrix of the mother we were the recipients of endowments and blessings of God, yet these were as nothing compared to the powers and graces bestowed upon us after birth into this human world. Likewise, if we are born from the matrix of this physical and phenomenal environment into the freedom and loftiness of the spiritual life and vision, we shall consider this mortal existence and its blessings as worthless by comparison.

In the spiritual world the divine bestowals are infinite, for in that realm there is neither separation nor disintegration, which characterize the world of material existence. Spiritual existence is absolute immortality, completeness and unchangeable being. Therefore, we must thank God that He has created for us both material blessings and spiritual bestowals. He has given us material gifts and spiritual graces, outer sight to view the lights of the sun and inner vision by which we may perceive the glory of God. He has designed the outer ear to enjoy the melodies of sound and the inner hearing wherewith we may hear the voice of our Creator. We must strive with energies of heart, soul and mind to develop and manifest the perfections and virtues latent within the realities of the phenomenal world, for the human reality may be compared to a seed. If we sow the seed, a mighty tree appears from it. The virtues of the seed are revealed in the tree; it puts forth branches, leaves, blossoms, and produces fruits. All these virtues were hidden and potential in the seed. Through the blessing and bounty of cultivation these virtues became apparent. Similarly, the merciful God, our Creator, has deposited within human realities certain latent and potential virtues. Through education and culture these virtues deposited by the loving God will become apparent in the human reality, even as the unfoldment of the tree from within the germinating seed.

'ABDU'L-BAHÁ 23

The greatest attainment in the world of humanity is nearness to God. Every lasting glory, honor, grace and beauty which comes to man comes through nearness to God. All the Prophets and apostles longed and prayed for nearness to the Creator. How many nights they passed in sleepless yearning for this station; how many days they devoted to supplication for this attainment, seeking ever to draw nigh unto Him! But nearness to God is not an easy accomplishment. During the time Jesus Christ was upon the earth mankind sought nearness to God, but in that day no one attained it save a very few—His disciples. Those blessed souls were confirmed with divine nearness through the love of God. Divine nearness is dependent upon attainment to the knowledge of God, upon severance from all else save God. It is contingent upon self-sacrifice and to be found only through forfeiting wealth and worldly possessions. It is made possible through the baptism of water and fire revealed in the Gospels. Water symbolizes the water of life, which is knowledge, and fire is the fire of the love of God; therefore, man must be baptized with the water of life, the Holy Spirit and the fire of the love of the Kingdom. Until he attains these three degrees, nearness to God is not possible. . . . And be it known that this nearness is not dependent upon time or place. Nearness to God is dependent upon purity of the heart and exhilaration of the spirit through the glad tidings of the Kingdom. Consider how a pure, well-polished mirror fully reflects the effulgence of the sun, no matter how distant the sun may be. As soon as the mirror is cleaned and purified, the sun will manifest itself. The more pure and sanctified the heart of man becomes, the nearer it draws to God, and the light of the Sun of Reality is revealed within it. This light sets hearts aglow with the fire of the love of God, opens in them the doors of knowledge and unseals the divine mysteries so that spiritual discoveries are made possible. All the Prophets have drawn near to God through severance. We must emulate those Holy Souls and renounce our own wishes and desires. We must purify ourselves from the mire and soil of earthly contact until our hearts become as mirrors in clearness and the light of the most great guidance reveals itself in them.

Bahá'u'lláh proclaims in the Hidden Words that God inspires His servants and is revealed through them. He says, "Thy heart is My home; sanctify it for My descent. Thy spirit is My place of revelation; cleanse it for My manifestation." Therefore, we learn that nearness to God is possible through devotion to Him, through entrance into the Kingdom and service to humanity; it is attained by unity with mankind and through loving-kindness to all; it is dependent upon investigation of truth, acquisition of praiseworthy virtues, service in the cause of universal peace and personal sanctification. In a word, nearness to God necessitates sacrifice of self, severance and the giving up of all to Him. Nearness is likeness.

Behold how the sun shines upon all creation, but only surfaces that are pure and polished can reflect its glory and light. The darkened soul has no portion of the revelation of the glorious effulgence of reality; and the soil of self, unable to take advantage of that light, does not produce growth. The eyes of the blind cannot behold the rays of the sun; only pure eyes with sound and perfect sight can receive them. Green and living trees can absorb the bounty of the sun; dead roots and withered branches are destroyed by it. Therefore, man must seek capacity and develop readiness. As long as he lacks susceptibility to divine influences, he is incapable of reflecting the light and assimilating its benefits. Sterile soil will produce nothing, even if the cloud of mercy pours rain upon it a thousand years. We must make the soil of our hearts receptive and fertile by tilling in order that the rain of divine mercy may refresh them and bring forth roses and hyacinths of heavenly planting. We must have perceiving eyes in order to see the light of the sun. We must cleanse the nostril in order to scent the fragrances of the divine rose garden. We must render the ears attentive in order to hear the summons of the supreme Kingdom.

No matter how beautiful the melody, the ear that is deaf cannot hear it, cannot receive the call of the Supreme Concourse. The nostril that is clogged with dust cannot inhale the fragrant odors of the blossoms. Therefore, we must ever strive for capacity and seek readiness. As long as we lack susceptibility, the beauties and bounties of God cannot penetrate. Christ spoke a parable in which He said His words were like the seeds of the sower; some fall upon stony ground, some upon sterile soil, some are choked by thorns and thistles, but some fall upon the ready, receptive and fertile ground of human hearts. When seeds are cast upon sterile soil, no growth follows. Those cast upon stony ground will grow a short time, but lacking deep roots will wither away. Thorns and thistles destroy others completely, but the seed cast in good ground brings forth harvest and fruitage.

In the same way, the words I speak to you here tonight may produce no effect whatever.[11] Some hearts may be affected, then soon forget; others owing to superstitious ideas and imaginations may even fail to hear and understand; but the blessed souls who are attentive to my exhortation and admonition, listening with the ear of acceptance, allowing my words to penetrate effectively, will advance day by day toward full fruition, yea even to the Supreme Concourse. Consider how the parable makes attainment dependent upon capacity. Unless capacity is developed, the summons of the Kingdom cannot reach the ear, the light of the Sun of Truth will not be observed, and the fragrances of the rose

---

11. 'Abdu'l-Bahá was speaking at the Mount Morris Baptist Church in New York City on 26 May 1912.

garden of inner significance will be lost. Let us endeavor to attain capacity, susceptibility and worthiness that we may hear the call of the glad tidings of the Kingdom, become revivified by the breaths of the Holy Spirit, hoist the standard of the oneness of humanity, establish human brotherhood, and under the protection of divine grace attain the everlasting and eternal life.

'ABDU'L-BAHÁ 24

You have asked why it was necessary for the soul that was from God to make this journey back to God? . . .

The reality underlying this question is that the evil spirit, Satan or whatever is interpreted as evil, refers to the lower nature in man. This baser nature is symbolized in various ways. In man there are two expressions: One is the expression of nature; the other, the expression of the spiritual realm. The world of nature is defective. Look at it clearly, casting aside all superstition and imagination. If you should leave a man uneducated and barbarous in the wilds of Africa, would there be any doubt about his remaining ignorant? God has never created an evil spirit; all such ideas and nomenclature are symbols expressing the mere human or earthly nature of man. It is an essential condition of the soil of earth that thorns, weeds and fruitless trees may grow from it. Relatively speaking, this is evil; it is simply the lower state and baser product of nature.

It is evident, therefore, that man is in need of divine education and inspiration, that the spirit and bounties of God are essential to his development. That is to say, the teachings of Christ and the Prophets are necessary for his education and guidance. Why? Because They are the divine Gardeners Who till the earth of human hearts and minds. They educate man, uproot the weeds, burn the thorns and remodel the waste places into gardens and orchards where fruitful trees grow. The wisdom and purpose of Their training is that man must pass from degree to degree of progressive unfoldment until perfection is attained. For instance, if a man should live his entire life in one city, he cannot gain a knowledge of the whole world. To become perfectly informed he must visit other cities, see the mountains and valleys, cross the rivers and traverse the plains. In other words, without progressive and universal education perfection will not be attained.

Man must walk in many paths and be subjected to various processes in his evolution upward. Physically he is not born in full stature but passes through consecutive stages of fetus, infant, childhood, youth, maturity and old age. Suppose he had the power to remain young throughout his life. He then would not understand the meaning of old age and could not believe it existed. If he could not realize the condition of old age, he would not know that he was young. He would not know the difference between young and old without experiencing the old. Unless you have passed through the state of infancy, how would you know this was an infant beside you? If there were no wrong, how would you recognize the right? If it were not for sin, how would you appreciate virtue? If evil deeds were unknown, how could you commend good actions? If sickness did not exist, how would you understand health? Evil is nonexistent; it is the absence of good. Sickness is the loss of health; poverty, the lack of riches. When wealth disappears, you are poor; you look within the treasure box but find nothing there. Without knowledge there is ignorance; therefore, ignorance is simply the lack of knowledge. Death is the absence of life. Therefore, on the one hand, we have existence; on the other, nonexistence, negation or absence of existence.

Briefly, the journey of the soul is necessary. The pathway of life is the road which leads to divine knowledge and attainment. Without training and guidance the soul could never progress beyond the conditions of its lower nature, which is ignorant and defective.
ʻAbduʼl-Bahá 25

"Does the soul progress more through sorrow or through the joy in this world?"

ʻAbduʼl-Baha.—"The mind and spirit of man advance when he is tried by suffering. The more the ground is ploughed the better the seed will grow, the better the harvest will be. Just as the plough furrows the earth deeply, purifying it of weeds and thistles, so suffering and tribulation free man from the petty affairs of this worldly life until he arrives at a state of complete detachment. His attitude in this world will be that of divine happiness. Man is, so to speak, unripe: the heat of the fire of suffering will mature him. Look back to the times past and you will find that the greatest men have suffered most."

"He who through suffering has attained development, should he fear happiness?"

ʻAbduʼl-Baha.—"Through suffering he will attain to an eternal happiness which nothing can take from him. The apostles of Christ suffered: they attained eternal happiness."

"Then it is impossible to attain happiness without suffering?"

'Abdu'l-Baha.—"To attain eternal happiness one must suffer. He who has reached the state of self-sacrifice has true joy. Temporal joy will vanish."

'ABDU'L-BAHÁ 26

Just as the effects and the fruitage of the uterine life are not to be found in that dark and narrow place, and only when the child is transferred to this wide earth do the benefits and uses of growth and development in that previous world become revealed—so likewise reward and punishment, heaven and hell, requital and retribution for actions done in this present life, will stand revealed in that other world beyond. And just as, if human life in the womb were limited to that uterine world, existence there would be nonsensical, irrelevant—so too if the life of this world, the deeds here done and their fruitage, did not come forth in the world beyond, the whole process would be irrational and foolish.

Know then that the Lord God possesseth invisible realms which the human intellect can never hope to fathom nor the mind of man conceive. When once thou hast cleansed the channel of thy spiritual sense from the pollution of this worldly life, then wilt thou breathe in the sweet scents of holiness that blow from the blissful bowers of that heavenly land.

'ABDU'L-BAHÁ 27

MEDITATIONS ON FREEING THE SOUL'S POTENTIAL

O SON OF MAN!

Veiled in My immemorial being and in the ancient eternity of My essence, I knew My love for thee; therefore I created thee, have engraved on thee Mine image and revealed to thee My beauty.

BAHÁ'U'LLÁH 28

O SON OF BEING!

With the hands of power I made thee and with the fingers of strength I created thee; and within thee have I placed the essence of My light. Be thou content with it and seek naught else, for My work is perfect and My command is binding. Question it not, nor have a doubt thereof.

BAHÁ'U'LLÁH 29

O SON OF BEING!

Thou art My lamp and My light is in thee. Get thou from it thy radiance and seek none other than Me. For I have created thee rich and have bountifully shed My favor upon thee.

BAHÁ'U'LLÁH 30

O SON OF MAN!

I loved thy creation, hence I created thee. Wherefore, do thou love Me, that I may name thy name and fill thy soul with the spirit of life.

BAHÁ'U'LLÁH 31

O SON OF UTTERANCE!
Thou art My stronghold; enter therein that thou mayest abide in safety. My love is in thee, know it, that thou mayest find Me near unto thee.

BAHÁ'U'LLÁH 32

O SON OF SPIRIT!
I created thee rich, why dost thou bring thyself down to poverty? Noble I made thee, wherewith dost thou abase thyself? Out of the essence of knowledge I gave thee being, why seekest thou enlightenment from anyone beside Me? Out of the clay of love I molded thee, how dost thou busy thyself with another? Turn thy sight unto thyself, that thou mayest find Me standing within thee, mighty, powerful and self-subsisting.

BAHÁ'U'LLÁH 33

O SON OF SPIRIT!
My first counsel is this: Possess a pure, kindly and radiant heart, that thine may be a sovereignty ancient, imperishable and ever-lasting.

BAHÁ'U'LLÁH 34

4

ETERNITY
LIFE
BEYOND
THIS
LIFE

THE WORLDS OF GOD

Know thou of a truth that the worlds of God are countless in their number, and infinite in their range. None can reckon or comprehend them except God, the All-Knowing, the All-Wise. Consider thy state when asleep. Verily, I say, this phenomenon is the most mysterious of the signs of God amongst men, were they to ponder it in their hearts. Behold how the thing which thou hast seen in thy dream is, after a considerable lapse of time, fully realized. Had the world in which thou didst find thyself in thy dream been identical with the world in which thou livest, it would have been necessary for the event occurring in that dream to have transpired in this world at the very moment of its occurrence. Were it so, you yourself would have borne witness unto it. This being not the case, however, it must necessarily follow that the world in which thou livest is different and apart from that which thou hast experienced in thy dream. This latter world hath neither beginning nor end. It would be true if thou wert to contend that this same world is, as decreed by the All-Glorious and Almighty God, within thy proper self and is wrapped up within thee. It would equally be true to maintain that thy spirit, having transcended the limitations of sleep and having stripped itself of all earthly attachment, hath, by the act of God, been made to traverse a realm which lieth hidden in the innermost reality of this world. Verily I say, the creation of God embraceth worlds besides this world, and creatures apart from these creatures. In each of these worlds He hath ordained things which none can search except Himself, the All-Searching, the All-Wise. Do thou meditate on that which We have revealed unto thee, that thou mayest discover the purpose of God, thy Lord, and the Lord of all worlds. In these words the mysteries of Divine Wisdom have been treasured.

Bahá'u'lláh 1

One of the created phenomena is the dream. Behold how many secrets are deposited therein, how many wisdoms treasured up, how many worlds concealed. Observe, how thou art asleep in a dwelling, and its doors are barred; on a sudden thou findest thyself in a far-off city, which thou enterest without moving thy feet or wearying thy body; without using thine eyes, thou seest; without taxing thine ears, thou hearest; without a tongue, thou speakest. And perchance when ten years are gone, thou wilt witness in the outer world the very things thou hast dreamed tonight.

Now there are many wisdoms to ponder in the dream. . . . First, what is this world, where without eye and ear and hand and tongue a man puts all of these to use? Second, how is it that in the outer world thou seest today the effect of a dream, when thou didst vision it in the world of sleep some ten years past? Consider the difference between these two worlds and the mysteries which they conceal, that thou mayest attain to divine confirmations and heavenly discoveries and enter the regions of holiness.

God, the Exalted, hath placed these signs in men, to the end that philosophers may not deny the mysteries of the life beyond nor belittle that which hath been promised them.

BAHÁ'U'LLÁH 2

Wert thou to ponder in thine heart the behavior of the Prophets of God thou wouldst assuredly and readily testify that there must needs be other worlds besides this world. The majority of the truly wise and learned have, throughout the ages, as it hath been recorded by the Pen of Glory in the Tablet of Wisdom, borne witness to the truth of that which the holy Writ of God hath revealed. Even the materialists have testified in their writings to the wisdom of these divinely-appointed Messengers, and have regarded the references made by the Prophets to Paradise, to hell fire, to future reward and punishment, to have been actuated by a desire to educate and uplift the souls of men. Consider, therefore, how the generality of mankind, whatever their beliefs or theories, have recognized the excellence, and admitted the superiority, of these Prophets of God. These Gems of Detachment are acclaimed by some as the embodiments of wisdom, while others believe them to be the mouthpiece of God Himself. How could such Souls have consented to surrender themselves unto their enemies if they believed all the worlds of God to have been reduced to this earthly life? Would they have willingly suffered such afflictions and torments as no man hath ever experienced or witnessed?

BAHÁ'U'LLÁH 3

THE NATURE OF THE WORLD BEYOND

The world beyond is as different from this world as this world is different from that of the child while still in the womb of its mother.

BAHÁ'U'LLÁH 4

The world of the Kingdom is the realm of divine bestowals and the bounties of God. It is attainment of the highest virtues of humanity; it is nearness to God; it is capacity to receive the bounties of the ancient Lord. When man advances to this station, he attains the second birth. Before his first or physical birth man was in the world of the matrix. He had no knowledge of this world; his eyes could not see; his ears could not hear. When he was born from the world of the matrix, he beheld another world. The sun was shining with its splendors, the moon radiant in the heavens, the stars twinkling in the expansive firmament, the seas surging, trees verdant and green, all kinds of creatures enjoying life here, infinite bounties prepared for him. In the world of the matrix none of these things existed. In that world he had no knowledge of this vast range of existence; nay, rather, he would have denied the reality of this world. But after his birth he began to open his eyes and behold the wonders of this illimitable universe. Similarly, as long as man is in the matrix of the human world, as long as he is the captive of nature, he is out of touch and without knowledge of the universe of the Kingdom. If he attains rebirth while in the world of nature, he will become informed of the divine world. He will observe that another and a higher world exists. Wonderful bounties descend; eternal life awaits; everlasting glory surrounds him. All the signs of reality and greatness are there. He will see the lights of God. All these experiences will be his when he is born out of the world of nature into the divine world.

'ABDU'L-BAHÁ 5

You question about eternal life and the entrance into the Kingdom. The outer expression used for the Kingdom is heaven; but this is a comparison and similitude, not a reality or fact, for the Kingdom is not a material place; it is sanctified from time and place. It is a spiritual world, a divine world, and the center of the Sovereignty of God; it is freed from body and that which is corporeal, and it is purified and sanctified from the imaginations of the human world. To be limited to place is a property of bodies and not of spirits. Place and time surround the body, not the mind and spirit. Observe that the body of man is confined to a small place; it covers only two spans of earth. But the spirit and mind of man travel to all countries and regions—even through the limitless space of the heavens—surround all that exists, and make discoveries in the exalted spheres and infinite distances. This is because the spirit has no place; it is placeless; and for the spirit the earth and the heaven are as one since it makes discoveries in both. But the body is limited to a place and does not know that which is beyond it. . . .

The meaning is that the life of the Kingdom is the life of the spirit, the eternal life, and that it is purified from place, like the spirit of man which has no place. For if you examine the human body, you will not find a special spot or locality for the spirit, for it has never had a place; it is immaterial. It has a connection with the body like that of the sun with this mirror. The sun is not within the mirror, but it has a connection with the mirror.

In the same way the world of the Kingdom is sanctified from everything that can be perceived by the eye or by the other senses—hearing, smell, taste or touch. The mind which is in man, the existence of which is recognized—where is it in him? If you examine the body with the eye, the ear or the other senses, you will not find it; nevertheless, it exists. Therefore, the mind has no place, but it is connected with the brain. The Kingdom is also like this. In the same way love has no place, but it is connected with the heart; so the Kingdom has no place, but is connected with man.

'ABDU'L-BAHÁ 6

The souls of the children of the Kingdom, after their separation from the body, ascend unto the realm of everlasting life. But if ye ask as to the place, know ye that the world of existence is a single world, although its stations are various and distinct. For example, the mineral life occupieth its own plane, but a mineral entity is without any awareness at all of the vegetable kingdom, and indeed, with its inner tongue denieth that there is any such kingdom. In the same way, a vegetable entity knoweth nothing of the animal world, remaining completely heedless and ignorant thereof, for the stage of the animal is higher than that of the vegetable, and the vegetable is veiled from the animal world and inwardly denieth the existence of that world—all this while animal, vegetable and mineral dwell together in the one world. In the same way the animal remaineth totally unaware of that power of the human mind which graspeth universal ideas and layeth bare the secrets of creation—so that a man who liveth in the east can make plans and arrangements for the west; can unravel mysteries; although located on the continent of Europe can discover America; although sited on the earth can lay hold of the inner realities of the stars of heaven. Of this power of discovery which belongeth to the human mind, this power which can grasp abstract and universal ideas, the animal remaineth totally ignorant, and indeed denieth its existence.

In the same way, the denizens of this earth are completely unaware of the world of the Kingdom and deny the existence thereof. They ask, for example: "Where is the Kingdom? Where is the Lord of the Kingdom?" These people are even as the mineral and the vegetable, who know nothing whatever of the animal and the human realm; they see it not; they find it not. Yet the mineral and vegetable, the animal and man, are all living here together in this world of existence.

. . . the tests and trials of God take place in this world, not in the world of the Kingdom.

. . . .

. . . the center of the Sun of Truth is in the supernal world— the Kingdom of God. Those souls who are pure and unsullied, upon the dissolution of their elemental frames, hasten away to the world of God, and that world is within this world. The people of this world, however, are unaware of that world, and are even as the mineral and the vegetable that know nothing of the world of the animal and the world of man.

'ABDU'L-BAHÁ 7

Those souls that, in this day, enter the divine kingdom and attain
everlasting life, although materially dwelling on earth, yet in
reality soar in the realm of heaven. Their bodies may linger on
earth, but their spirits travel in the immensity of space. For as
thoughts widen and become illumined, they acquire the power
of flight and transport man to the kingdom of God.

'ABDU'L-BAHÁ 8

Concerning the future life what Bahá'u'lláh says is that the soul
will continue to ascend through many worlds. What those
worlds are and what their nature is we cannot know. The same
way that the child in the matrix cannot know this world so we
cannot know what the other world is going to be.

SHOGHI EFFENDI 9

You ask an explanation of what happens to us after we leave this
world: This is a question which none of the Prophets have ever
answered in detail, for the very simple reason that you cannot
convey to a person's mind something entirely different from
everything they have ever experienced. 'Abdu'l-Bahá gave the
wonderful example of the relation of this life to the next life being
like the child in the womb; it develops eyes, ears, hands, feet, a
tongue, and yet it has nothing to see or hear, it cannot walk or
grasp things or speak; all these faculties it is developing for this
world. If you tried to explain to an embryo what this world is like
it could never understand—but it understands when it is born,
and its faculties can be used. So we cannot picture our state in the
next world. All we know is that our consciousness, our person-

ality, endures in some new state, and that that world is as much better than this one as this one is better than the dark womb of our mother was. . . .

SHOGHI EFFENDI 10

THE SOUL AFTER DEATH

When the soul attaineth the Presence of God, it will assume the form that best befitteth its immortality and is worthy of its celestial habitation. Such an existence is a contingent and not an absolute existence, inasmuch as the former is preceded by a cause, whilst the latter is independent thereof. Absolute existence is strictly confined to God, exalted be His glory.

BAHÁ'U'LLÁH 11

And now concerning thy question regarding the soul of man and its survival after death. Know thou of a truth that the soul, after its separation from the body, will continue to progress until it attaineth the presence of God, in a state and condition which neither the revolution of ages and centuries, nor the changes and chances of this world, can alter. It will endure as long as the Kingdom of God, His sovereignty, His dominion and power will endure. It will manifest the signs of God and His attributes, and will reveal His loving-kindness and bounty. The movement of My Pen is stilled when it attempteth to befittingly describe the loftiness and glory of so exalted a station. The honor with which the Hand of Mercy will invest the soul is such as no tongue can

adequately reveal, nor any other earthly agency describe. Blessed
is the soul which, at the hour of its separation from the body, is
sanctified from the vain imaginings of the peoples of the world.
Such a soul liveth and moveth in accordance with the Will of its
Creator, and entereth the all-highest Paradise. The Maids of
Heaven, inmates of the loftiest mansions, will circle around it,
and the Prophets of God and His chosen ones will seek its companionship. With them that soul will freely converse, and will
recount unto them that which it hath been made to endure in the
path of God, the Lord of all worlds. If any man be told that which
hath been ordained for such a soul in the worlds of God, the Lord
of the throne on high and of earth below, his whole being will
instantly blaze out in his great longing to attain that most exalted,
that sanctified and resplendent station. . . .

BAHÁ'U'LLÁH 12

Thou hast . . . asked Me concerning the state of the soul after its
separation from the body. Know thou, of a truth, that if the soul
of man hath walked in the ways of God, it will, assuredly, return
and be gathered to the glory of the Beloved. By the righteousness
of God! It shall attain a station such as no pen can depict, or
tongue describe. The soul that hath remained faithful to the
Cause of God, and stood unwaveringly firm in His Path shall,
after his ascension, be possessed of such power that all the worlds
which the Almighty hath created can benefit through him. Such
a soul provideth, at the bidding of the Ideal King and Divine
Educator, the pure leaven that leaveneth the world of being, and
furnisheth the power through which the arts and wonders of the

world are made manifest. Consider how meal needeth leaven to be leavened with. Those souls that are the symbols of detachment are the leaven of the world. Meditate on this, and be of the thankful.

BAHÁ'U'LLÁH 13

The nature of the soul after death can never be described, nor is it meet and permissible to reveal its whole character to the eyes of men. The Prophets and Messengers of God have been sent down for the sole purpose of guiding mankind to the straight Path of Truth. The purpose underlying Their revelation hath been to educate all men, that they may, at the hour of death, ascend, in the utmost purity and sanctity and with absolute detachment, to the throne of the Most High. The light which these souls radiate is responsible for the progress of the world and the advancement of its peoples. They are like unto leaven which leaveneth the world of being, and constitute the animating force through which the arts and wonders of the world are made manifest. Through them the clouds rain their bounty upon men, and the earth bringeth forth its fruits. All things must needs have a cause, a motive power, an animating principle. These souls and symbols of detachment have provided, and will continue to provide, the supreme moving impulse in the world of being.

BAHÁ'U'LLÁH 14

Thou hast asked Me whether man, as apart from the Prophets of God and His chosen ones, will retain, after his physical death, the self-same individuality, personality, consciousness, and understanding that characterize his life in this world. If this should be the case, how is it, thou hast observed, that whereas such slight injuries to his mental faculties as fainting and severe illness deprive him of his understanding and consciousness, his death, which must involve the decomposition of his body and the dissolution of its elements, is powerless to destroy that understanding and extinguish that consciousness? How can any one imagine that man's consciousness and personality will be maintained, when the very instruments necessary to their existence and function will have completely disintegrated?

Know thou that the soul of man is exalted above, and is independent of all infirmities of body or mind. That a sick person showeth signs of weakness is due to the hindrances that interpose themselves between his soul and his body, for the soul itself remaineth unaffected by any bodily ailments. Consider the light of the lamp. Though an external object may interfere with its radiance, the light itself continueth to shine with undiminished power. In like manner, every malady afflicting the body of man is an impediment that preventeth the soul from manifesting its inherent might and power. When it leaveth the body, however, it will evince such ascendancy, and reveal such influence as no force on earth can equal. Every pure, every refined and sanctified soul will be endowed with tremendous power, and shall rejoice with exceeding gladness.

Consider the lamp which is hidden under a bushel. Though its light be shining, yet its radiance is concealed from men. Likewise, consider the sun which hath been obscured by the clouds. Observe how its splendor appeareth to have diminished, when in reality the source of that light hath remained unchanged. The soul of man should be likened unto this sun, and all things on earth should be regarded as his body. So long as no external impediment interveneth between them, the body will, in its entirety, continue to reflect the light of the soul, and to be sustained by its power. As soon as, however, a veil interposeth itself between them, the brightness of that light seemeth to lessen.

Consider again the sun when it is completely hidden behind the clouds. Though the earth is still illumined with its light, yet the measure of light which it receiveth is considerably reduced. Not until the clouds have dispersed, can the sun shine again in the plenitude of its glory. Neither the presence of the cloud nor its absence can, in any way, affect the inherent splendor of the sun. The soul of man is the sun by which his body is illumined, and from which it draweth its sustenance, and should be so regarded.

BAHÁ'U'LLÁH 15

In the other world the human reality doth not assume a physical form, rather doth it take on a heavenly form, made up of elements of that heavenly realm.

'ABDU'L-BAHÁ 16

Some think that the body is the substance and exists by itself, and that the spirit is accidental and depends upon the substance of the body, although, on the contrary, the rational soul is the substance, and the body depends upon it. If the accident—that is to say, the body—be destroyed, the substance, the spirit, remains.

Second, the rational soul, meaning the human spirit, does not descend into the body—that is to say, it does not enter it, for descent and entrance are characteristics of bodies, and the rational soul is exempt from this. The spirit never entered this body, so in quitting it, it will not be in need of an abiding-place: no, the spirit is connected with the body, as this light is with this mirror. When the mirror is clear and perfect, the light of the lamp will be apparent in it, and when the mirror becomes covered with dust or breaks, the light will disappear.

The rational soul—that is to say, the human spirit—has neither entered this body nor existed through it; so after the disintegration of the composition of the body, how should it be in need of a substance through which it may exist? On the contrary, the rational soul is the substance through which the body exists. The personality of the rational soul is from its beginning; it is not due to the instrumentality of the body, but the state and the personality of the rational soul may be strengthened in this world; it will make progress and will attain to the degrees of perfection, or it will remain in the lowest abyss of ignorance, veiled and deprived from beholding the signs of God.

'ABDU'L-BAHÁ 17

Bodily cold and heat cannot affect the spirit, for it is warmed by the fire of the Love of God. When we understand this, we begin to understand something of our life in the world to come.

God, in His Bounty, has given us a foretaste here, has given us certain proofs of the difference that exists between body, soul and spirit.

We see that cold, heat, suffering, etc, only concern the *body,* they do not touch the spirit.

How often do we see a man, poor, sick, miserably clad, and with no means of support, yet spiritually strong. Whatever his body has to suffer, his spirit is free and well! Again, how often do we see a rich man, physically strong and healthy, but with a soul sick unto death.

It is quite apparent to the seeing mind that a man's spirit is something very different from his physical body.

The spirit is changeless, indestructible. The progress and development of the soul, the joy and sorrow of the soul, are independent of the physical body.

If we are caused joy or pain by a friend, if a love prove true or false, it is the soul that is affected. If our dear ones are far from us—it is the soul that grieves, and the grief or trouble of the soul may react on the body.

Thus, when the spirit is fed with holy virtues, then is the body joyous; if the soul falls into sin, the body is in torment!

When we find truth, constancy, fidelity, and love, we are happy; but if we meet with lying, faithlessness, and deceit, we are miserable.

These are all things pertaining to the soul, and are not *bodily* ills. Thus, it is apparent that the soul, even as the body, has its own individuality. But if the body undergoes a change, the spirit need not be touched. When you break a glass on which the sun shines, the glass is broken, but the sun still shines! If a cage containing a bird is destroyed, the bird is unharmed! If a lamp is broken, the flame can still burn bright!

The same thing applies to the spirit of man. Though death destroy his body, it has no power over his spirit—this is eternal, everlasting, both birthless and deathless.

As to the soul of man after death, it remains in the degree of purity to which it has evolved during life in the physical body, and after it is freed from the body it remains plunged in the ocean of God's Mercy.

From the moment the soul leaves the body and arrives in the Heavenly World, its evolution is spiritual, and that evolution is: *The approaching unto God.*

In the physical creation, evolution is from one degree of perfection to another. The mineral passes with its mineral perfections to the vegetable; the vegetable, with its perfections, passes to the animal world, and so on to that of humanity. This world is full of seeming contradictions; in each of these kingdoms (mineral, vegetable and animal) life exists in its degree; though when compared to the life in a man, the earth appears to be dead, yet she, too, lives and has a life of her own. In this world things live and die, and live again in other forms of life, but in the world of the spirit it is quite otherwise.

The soul does not evolve from degree to degree as a law— it only evolves nearer to God, by the Mercy and Bounty of God.

It is my earnest prayer that we may all be in the Kingdom of God, and near Him.

'ABDU'L-BAHÁ 18

As the spirit continues to exist after death, it necessarily progresses or declines; and in the other world to cease to progress is the same as to decline; but it never leaves its own condition, in which it continues to develop. For example, the reality of the spirit of Peter, however far it may progress, will not reach to the condition of the Reality of Christ; it progresses only in its own environment.

Look at this mineral. However far it may evolve, it only evolves in its own condition; you cannot bring the crystal to a state where it can attain to sight. This is impossible. So the moon which is in the heavens, however far it might evolve, could never become a luminous sun, but in its own condition it has apogee and perigee. However far the disciples might progress, they could never become Christ. It is true that coal could become a diamond, but both are in the mineral condition, and their component elements are the same.

'ABDU'L-BAHÁ 19

Tonight I will speak of the evolution or progress of the spirit.[1]

Absolute repose does not exist in nature. All things either make progress or lose ground. Everything moves forward or backward, nothing is without motion. From his birth, a man progresses physically until he reaches maturity, then, having arrived at the prime of his life, he begins to decline, the strength and powers of his body decrease, and he gradually arrives at the hour of death. Likewise a plant progresses from the seed to maturity, then its life begins to lessen until it fades and dies. A bird soars to a certain height and having reached the highest possible point in its flight, begins its descent to earth.

Thus it is evident that movement is essential to all existence. All material things progress to a certain point, then begin to decline. This is the law which governs the whole physical creation.

---

1. From a talk 'Abdu'l-Bahá gave in Paris on 10 November 1911.

Now let us consider the soul. We have seen that movement is essential to existence; nothing that has life is without motion. All creation, whether of the mineral, vegetable or animal kingdom, is compelled to obey the law of motion; it must either ascend or descend. But with the human soul, there is no decline. Its only movement is towards perfection; growth and progress alone constitute the motion of the soul.

Divine perfection is infinite, therefore the progress of the soul is also infinite. From the very birth of a human being the soul progresses, the intellect grows and knowledge increases. When the body dies the soul lives on. All the differing degrees of created physical beings are limited, but the soul is limitless!

In all religions the belief exists that the soul survives the death of the body. Intercessions are sent up for the beloved dead, prayers are said for their progress and for the forgiveness of their sins. If the soul perished with the body all this would have no meaning. Further, if it were not possible for the soul to advance towards perfection after it had been released from the body, of what avail are all these loving prayers, of devotion?

We read in the sacred writings that "all good works are found again."[2] Now, if the soul did not survive, this also would mean nothing!

The very fact that our spiritual instinct, surely never given in vain, prompts us to pray for the welfare of those, our loved ones, who have passed out of the material world: does it not bear witness to the continuance of their existence?

---

2. i.e.—All good actions bring their own reward.

In the world of spirit there is no retrogression. The world of mortality is a world of contradictions, of opposites; motion being compulsory everything must either go forward or retreat. In the realm of spirit there is no retreat possible, all movement is bound to be towards a perfect state. "Progress" is the expression of spirit in the world of matter. The intelligence of man, his reasoning powers, his knowledge, his scientific achievements, all these being manifestations of the spirit, partake of the inevitable law of spiritual progress and are, therefore, of necessity, immortal.

My hope for you is that you will progress in the world of spirit, as well as in the world of matter; that your intelligence will develop, your knowledge will augment, and your understanding be widened.

You must ever press forward, never standing still; avoid stagnation, the first step to a backward movement, to decay.

'Abdu'l-Bahá 20

Question.—Through what means will the spirit of man—that is to say, the rational soul—after departing from this mortal world, make progress?

Answer.—The progress of man's spirit in the divine world, after the severance of its connection with the body of dust, is through the bounty and grace of the Lord alone, or through the intercession and the sincere prayers of other human souls, or through the charities and important good works which are performed in its name.

'Abdu'l-Bahá 21

Concerning your question whether a soul can receive knowledge of the Truth in the world beyond. Such knowledge is surely possible, and is but a sign of the loving mercy of the Almighty. We can, through our prayers, help every soul to gradually attain this high station, even if it has failed to reach it in this world. The progress of the soul does not come to an end with death. It rather starts along a new line. Bahá'u'lláh teaches that great and far-reaching possibilities await the soul in the other world. Spiritual progress in that realm is infinite, and no man, while on this earth, can visualize its full power and extent.

SHOGHI EFFENDI 22

MEDITATIONS ON LIFE BEYOND THIS LIFE

O SON OF MAN!

My eternity is My creation, I have created it for thee. Make it the garment of thy temple. My unity is My handiwork; I have wrought it for thee; clothe thyself therewith, that thou mayest be to all eternity the revelation of My everlasting being.

BAHÁ'U'LLÁH 23

O SON OF BEING!

Thy Paradise is My love; thy heavenly home, reunion with Me. Enter therein and tarry not. This is that which hath been destined for thee in Our kingdom above and Our exalted dominion.

BAHÁ'U'LLÁH 24

O SON OF MAN!
If thou lovest Me, turn away from thyself; and if thou seekest My pleasure, regard not thine own; that thou mayest die in Me and I may eternally live in thee.

BAHÁ'U'LLÁH 25

O COMPANION OF MY THRONE!
. . . Live . . . the days of thy life, that are less than a fleeting moment, with thy mind stainless, thy heart unsullied, thy thoughts pure, and thy nature sanctified, so that, free and content, thou mayest put away this mortal frame, and repair unto the mystic paradise and abide in the eternal kingdom for evermore.

BAHÁ'U'LLÁH 26

O SON OF MY HANDMAID!
Didst thou behold immortal sovereignty, thou wouldst strive to pass from this fleeting world. But to conceal the one from thee and to reveal the other is a mystery which none but the pure in heart can comprehend.

BAHÁ'U'LLÁH 27

O SON OF MAN!
Ascend unto My heaven, that thou mayest obtain the joy of reunion, and from the chalice of imperishable glory quaff the peerless wine.

BAHÁ'U'LLÁH 28

5

THIS LIFE AND
THE NEXT
DISCOVERIES,
ASSOCIATION,
AND
COMMUNICATION

SPIRITUAL DISCOVERIES IN THIS WORLD AND THE NEXT

Know thou that, according to what thy Lord, the Lord of all men, hath decreed in His Book, the favors vouchsafed by Him unto mankind have been, and will ever remain, limitless in their range. First and foremost among these favors, which the Almighty hath conferred upon man, is the gift of understanding. His purpose in conferring such a gift is none other except to enable His creature to know and recognize the one true God— exalted be His glory. This gift giveth man the power to discern the truth in all things, leadeth him to that which is right, and helpeth him to discover the secrets of creation.

BAHÁ'U'LLÁH 1

Thou didst write as to the question of spiritual discoveries. The spirit of man is a circumambient power that encompasseth the realities of all things. Whatsoever thou dost see about thee— wondrous products of human workmanship, inventions, discoveries and like evidences—each one of these was once a secret hidden away in the realm of the unknown. The human spirit laid that secret bare, and drew it forth from the unseen into the visible world. There is, for example, the power of steam, and photography and the phonograph, and wireless telegraphy, and advances in mathematics: each and every one of these was once a mystery, a closely guarded secret, yet the human spirit unraveled these secrets and brought them out of the invisible into the light of day. Thus is it clear that the human spirit is an all-encompassing power that exerteth its dominion over the inner essences of all created things, uncovering the well kept mysteries of the phenomenal world.

The divine spirit, however, doth unveil divine realities and universal mysteries that lie within the spiritual world. It is my hope that thou wilt attain unto this divine spirit, so that thou mayest uncover the secrets of the other world, as well as the mysteries of the world below.

'ABDU'L-BAHÁ 2

The reality of man embraces the realities of things, and discovers the verities, properties and secrets of things. So all these arts, wonders, sciences and knowledge have been discovered by the human reality. At one time these sciences, knowledge, wonders and arts were hidden and concealed secrets; then gradually the human reality discovered them and brought them from the realm of the invisible to the plane of the visible. Therefore, it is evident that the reality of man embraces things. Thus it is in Europe and discovers America; it is on the earth, and it makes discoveries in the heavens. It is the revealer of the secrets of things, and it is the knower of the realities of that which exists. These discoveries corresponding to the reality are similar to revelation, which is spiritual comprehension, divine inspiration and the association of human spirits. For instance, the Prophet says, "I saw, I said, I heard such a thing." It is, therefore, evident that the spirit has great perception without the intermediary of any of the five senses, such as the eyes or ears. Among spiritual souls there are spiritual understandings, discoveries, a communion which is purified from imagination and fancy, an association which is sanctified from time and place. So it is written in the Gospel that, on Mount Tabor, Moses and Elias came to Christ, and it is evident that this was not a material meeting. It was a spiritual condition which is expressed as a physical meeting.

The other sort of converse, presence and communications of spirits is but imagination and fancy, which only appears to have reality.

The mind and the thought of man sometimes discover truths, and from this thought and discovery signs and results are produced. This thought has a foundation. But many things come to the mind of man which are like the waves of the sea of imaginations; they have no fruit, and no result comes from them. In the same way, man sees in the world of sleep a vision which becomes exactly realized; at another time, he sees a dream which has absolutely no result.

What we mean is that this state, which we call the converse and communications of spirits, is of two kinds: one is simply imaginary, and the other is like the visions which are mentioned in the Holy Book, such as the revelations of St. John and Isaiah and the meeting of Christ with Moses and Elias. These are real, and produce wonderful effects in the minds and thoughts of men, and cause their hearts to be attracted.

'ABDU'L-BAHÁ 3

As to thy question regarding discoveries made by the soul after it hath put off its human form: certainly, that world is a world of perceptions and discoveries, for the interposed veil will be lifted away and the human spirit will gaze upon souls that are above, below, and on a par with itself. It is similar to the condition of a human being in the womb, where his eyes are veiled, and all things are hidden away from him. Once he is born out of the uterine world and entereth this life, he findeth it, with relation to that of the womb, to be a place of perceptions and discoveries, and he observeth all things through his outer eye. In the same way, once he hath departed this life, he will behold, in that world whatsoever was hidden from him here: but there he will look upon and comprehend all things with his inner eye. There will he gaze on his fellows and his peers, and those in the ranks above him, and those below.

'ABDU'L-BAHÁ 4

Consider how a being, in the world of the womb, was deaf of ear and blind of eye, and mute of tongue; how he was bereft of any perceptions at all. But once, out of that world of darkness, he passed into this world of light, then his eye saw, his ear heard, his tongue spoke. In the same way, once he hath hastened away from this mortal place into the Kingdom of God, then he will be born in the spirit; then the eye of his perception will open, the ear of his soul will hearken, and all the truths of which he was ignorant before will be made plain and clear.

'ABDU'L-BAHÁ 5

ASSOCIATION AND COMMUNICATION IN THIS LIFE AND THE NEXT

Concerning thy question whether human souls continue to be conscious one of another after their separation from the body. Know thou that the souls of the people of Bahá, who have entered and been established within the Crimson Ark, shall associate and commune intimately one with another, and shall be so closely associated in their lives, their aspirations, their aims and strivings as to be even as one soul. They are indeed the ones who are well-informed, who are keen-sighted, and who are endued with understanding. Thus hath it been decreed by Him Who is the All-Knowing, the All-Wise.

The people of Bahá, who are the inmates of the Ark of God, are, one and all, well aware of one another's state and condition, and are united in the bonds of intimacy and fellowship. Such a state, however, must depend upon their faith and their conduct. They that are of the same grade and station are fully aware of one another's capacity, character, accomplishments and merits. They that are of a lower grade, however, are incapable of comprehending adequately the station, or of estimating the merits, of those that rank above them. Each shall receive his share from thy Lord. Blessed is the man that hath turned his face towards God, and walked steadfastly in His love, until his soul hath winged its flight unto God, the Sovereign Lord of all, the Most Powerful, the Ever-Forgiving, the All-Merciful.

The souls of the infidels, however, shall . . . when breathing their last be made aware of the good things that have escaped them, and shall bemoan their plight, and shall humble themselves before God. They shall continue doing so after the separation of their souls from their bodies.

It is clear and evident that all men shall, after their physical death, estimate the worth of their deeds, and realize all that their hands have wrought. I swear by the Daystar that shineth above the horizon of Divine power! They that are the followers of the one true God shall, the moment they depart out of this life, experience such joy and gladness as would be impossible to describe, while they that live in error shall be seized with such fear and trembling, and shall be filled with such consternation, as nothing can exceed. Well is it with him that hath quaffed the choice and incorruptible wine of faith through the gracious favor and the manifold bounties of Him Who is the Lord of all Faiths. . . .

BAHÁ'U'LLÁH 6

The mysteries of which man is heedless in the earthly world, those will he discover in the heavenly world, and there will he be informed of the secrets of the truth; how much more will he recognize or discover persons with whom he has been associated. Undoubtedly, the holy souls who find a pure eye and are favored with insight will, in the kingdom of lights, be acquainted with all mysteries, and will seek the bounty of witnessing the reality of every great soul. They will even manifestly behold the beauty of God in that world. Likewise, will they find all the friends of God, both those of the former and recent times, present in the heavenly assemblage.

The difference and distinction between men will naturally become realized after their departure from this mortal world. But this distinction is not in respect to place, but in respect to the soul and conscience. For the Kingdom of God is sanctified (or free) from time and place; it is another world and another universe. And know thou for a certainty that in the divine worlds the spiritual beloved ones will recognize one another, and will seek union with each other, but a spiritual union. Likewise, a love that one may have entertained for anyone will not be forgotten in the world of the Kingdom, nor wilt thou forget there the life that thou hadst in the material world.

'ABDU'L-BAHÁ 7

"Can a departed soul converse with someone still on earth?"

'Abdu'l-Bahá.—"A conversation can be held, but not as our conversation. There is no doubt that the forces of the higher worlds interplay with the forces of this plane. The heart of man is open to inspiration; this is spiritual communication. As in a dream one talks with a friend while the mouth is silent, so is it in the conversation of the spirit. A man may converse with the ego within him saying: 'May I do this? Would it be advisable for me to do this work?' Such as this is conversation with the higher self."

'ABDU'L-BAHÁ 8

To tamper with psychic forces while in this world interferes with the condition of the soul in the world to come. These forces are real, but, normally, are not active on this plane. The child in the womb has its eyes, ears, hands, feet, etc., but they are not in activity. The whole purpose of life in the material world is the coming forth into the world of reality, where those forces will become active. They belong to that world.

'ABDU'L-BAHÁ 9

According to Bahá'u'lláh the soul retains its individuality and consciousness after death, and is able to commune with other souls. This communion, however, is purely spiritual in character, and is conditioned upon the disinterested and selfless love of the individuals for each other.

SHOGHI EFFENDI 10

INTERCEDING FOR THOSE IN THE NEXT WORLD

The wealth of the other world is nearness to God. Consequently, it is certain that those who are near the Divine Court are allowed to intercede, and this intercession is approved by God. But intercession in the other world is not like intercession in this world. It is another thing, another reality, which cannot be expressed in words.

If a wealthy man at the time of his death bequeaths a gift to the poor and miserable, and gives a part of his wealth to be spent for them, perhaps this action may be the cause of his pardon and forgiveness, and of his progress in the Divine Kingdom.

Also a father and mother endure the greatest troubles and

hardships for their children; and often when the children have reached the age of maturity, the parents pass on to the other world. Rarely does it happen that a father and mother in this world see the reward of the care and trouble they have undergone for their children. Therefore, children, in return for this care and trouble, must show forth charity and beneficence, and must implore pardon and forgiveness for their parents. So you ought, in return for the love and kindness shown you by your father, to give to the poor for his sake, with greatest submission and humility implore pardon and remission of sins, and ask for the supreme mercy.

It is even possible that the condition of those who have died in sin and unbelief may become changed—that is to say, they may become the object of pardon through the bounty of God, not through His justice—for bounty is giving without desert, and justice is giving what is deserved. As we have power to pray for these souls here, so likewise we shall possess the same power in the other world, which is the Kingdom of God. Are not all the people in that world the creatures of God? Therefore, in that world also they can make progress. As here they can receive light by their supplications, there also they can plead for forgiveness and receive light through entreaties and supplications. Thus as souls in this world, through the help of the supplications, the entreaties and the prayers of the holy ones, can acquire development, so is it the same after death. Through their own prayers and supplications they can also progress, more especially when they are the object of the intercession of the Holy Manifestations.

'ABDU'L-BAHÁ 11

Those who have ascended have different attributes from those who are still on earth, yet there is no real separation.

In prayer there is a mingling of station, a mingling of condition. Pray for them as they pray for you!

'ABDU'L-BAHÁ 12

MEDITATIONS ON DISCOVERIES, ASSOCIATION, AND COMMUNICATION

O SON OF WORLDLINESS!

Pleasant is the realm of being, wert thou to attain thereto; glorious is the domain of eternity, shouldst thou pass beyond the world of mortality; sweet is the holy ecstasy if thou drinkest of the mystic chalice from the hands of the celestial Youth. Shouldst thou attain this station, thou wouldst be freed from destruction and death, from toil and sin.

BAHÁ'U'LLÁH 13

O MOVING FORM OF DUST!

I desire communion with thee, but thou wouldst put no trust in Me. The sword of thy rebellion hath felled the tree of thy hope. At all times I am near unto thee, but thou art ever far from Me. Imperishable glory I have chosen for thee, yet boundless shame thou hast chosen for thyself. While there is yet time, return, and lose not thy chance.

BAHÁ'U'LLÁH 14

O SON OF EARTH!

Know, verily, the heart wherein the least remnant of envy yet lingers, shall never attain My everlasting dominion, nor inhale the sweet savors of holiness breathing from My kingdom of sanctity.

BAHÁ'U'LLÁH 15

O MY FRIENDS!

Quench ye the lamp of error, and kindle within your hearts the everlasting torch of divine guidance. For ere long the assayers of mankind shall, in the holy presence of the Adored, accept naught but purest virtue and deeds of stainless holiness.

BAHÁ'U'LLÁH 16

O OFFSPRING OF DUST!

Be not content with the ease of a passing day, and deprive not thyself of everlasting rest. Barter not the garden of eternal delight for the dust-heap of a mortal world. Up from thy prison ascend unto the glorious meads above, and from thy mortal cage wing thy flight unto the paradise of the Placeless.

BAHÁ'U'LLÁH 17

6

PRAYERS
AND
MEDITATIONS
FOR
SPIRITUAL
PROGRESS

INTERCESSIONS
FOR THE DEPARTED

(The Prayer for the Dead is to be used for Bahá'ís over the age of fifteen. "It is the only Bahá'í obligatory prayer which is to be recited in congregation; it is to be recited by one believer while all present stand. There is no requirement to face the Qiblih when reciting this prayer."—A Synopsis and Codification of the Kitáb-i-Aqdas)

O my God! This is Thy servant and the son of Thy servant who hath believed in Thee and in Thy signs, and set his face towards Thee, wholly detached from all except Thee. Thou art, verily, of those who show mercy the most merciful.

Deal with him, O Thou Who forgivest the sins of men and concealest their faults, as beseemeth the heaven of Thy bounty and the ocean of Thy grace. Grant him admission within the precincts of Thy transcendent mercy that was before the foundation of earth and heaven. There is no God but Thee, the Ever-Forgiving, the Most Generous.

Let him, then, repeat six times the greeting "Alláh-u-Abhá," and then repeat nineteen times each of the following verses:[1]

---

1. *The Kitáb-i-Aqdas* (note 11) clarifies the application of these instructions, indicating that each repetition of the greeting "Alláh-u-Abhá" is to be succeeded by nineteen repetitions of one of the six verses that follow.

We all, verily, worship God.

We all, verily, bow down before God.

We all, verily, are devoted unto God.

We all, verily, give praise unto God.

We all, verily, yield thanks unto God.

We all, verily, are patient in God.

(If the dead be a woman, let him say: This is Thy handmaiden and the daughter of Thy handmaiden, etc. . . .)

BAHÁ'U'LLÁH 1

Glory be to Thee, O Lord my God! I implore Thee by Thy Name, through which Thou didst lift up the ensigns of Thy guidance, and didst shed the radiance of Thy loving-kindness, and didst reveal the sovereignty of Thy Lordship; through which the lamp of Thy names hath appeared within the niche of Thine attributes, and He Who is the Tabernacle of Thy unity and the Manifestation of detachment hath shone forth; through which the ways of Thy guidance were made known, and the paths of Thy good pleasure were marked out; through which the foundations of error have been made to tremble, and the signs of wickedness have been abolished; through which the fountains of wisdom have burst forth, and the heavenly table hath been sent down; through which Thou didst preserve Thy servants and didst vouchsafe Thy healing; through which Thou didst show forth Thy tender mercies unto Thy servants and revealedst Thy forgiveness amidst Thy creatures—I implore Thee to keep safe him who hath held fast and returned unto Thee, and clung to Thy mercy, and seized the hem of Thy loving providence. Send down, then, upon him Thy healing, and make him whole, and endue him with a constancy vouchsafed by Thee, and a tranquillity bestowed by Thy highness.

Thou art, verily, the Healer, the Preserver, the Helper, the Almighty, the Powerful, the All-Glorious, the All-Knowing.

BAHÁ'U'LLÁH 2

Praised be Thou, O Lord my God! This is Thy servant who hath quaffed from the hands of Thy grace the wine of Thy tender mercy, and tasted of the savor of Thy love in Thy days. I beseech Thee, by the embodiments of Thy names whom no grief can hinder from rejoicing in Thy love or from gazing on Thy face, and whom all the hosts of the heedless are powerless to cause to turn aside from the path of Thy pleasure, to supply him with the good things Thou dost possess, and to raise him up to such heights that he will regard the world even as a shadow that vanisheth swifter than the twinkling of an eye.

Keep him safe also, O my God, by the power of Thine immeasurable majesty, from all that Thou abhorrest. Thou art, verily, his Lord and the Lord of all worlds.

BAHÁ'U'LLÁH 3

O my God, the God of bounty and mercy! Thou art that King by Whose commanding word the whole creation hath been called into being; and Thou art that All-Bountiful One the doings of Whose servants have never hindered Him from showing forth His grace, nor have they frustrated the revelations of His bounty.

Suffer this servant, I beseech Thee, to attain unto that which is the cause of his salvation in every world of Thy worlds. Thou art, verily, the Almighty, the Most Powerful, the All-Knowing, the All-Wise.

BAHÁ'U'LLÁH 4

Glory be to Thee, O Lord my God! Abase not him whom Thou hast exalted through the power of Thine everlasting sovereignty, and remove not far from Thee him whom Thou hast caused to enter the tabernacle of Thine eternity. Wilt Thou cast away, O my God, him whom Thou hast overshadowed with Thy Lordship, and wilt Thou turn away from Thee, O my Desire, him to whom Thou hast been a refuge? Canst Thou degrade him whom Thou hast uplifted, or forget him whom Thou didst enable to remember Thee?

Glorified, immensely glorified art Thou! Thou art He Who from everlasting hath been the King of the entire creation and its Prime Mover, and Thou wilt to everlasting remain the Lord of all created things and their Ordainer. Glorified art Thou, O my God! If Thou ceasest to be merciful unto Thy servants, who, then, will show mercy unto them; and if Thou refusest to succor Thy loved ones, who is there that can succor them?

Glorified, immeasurably glorified art Thou! Thou art adored in Thy truth, and Thee do we all, verily, worship; and Thou art manifest in Thy justice, and to Thee do we all, verily, bear witness. Thou art, in truth, beloved in Thy grace. No God is there but Thee, the Help in Peril, the Self-Subsisting.

BAHÁ'U'LLÁH 5

He is God, exalted is He, the Lord of loving-kindness and bounty!

Glory be unto Thee, Thou, O my God, the Lord Omnipotent. I testify to Thine omnipotence and Thy might, Thy sovereignty and Thy loving-kindness, Thy grace and Thy power, the oneness of Thy Being and the unity of Thine Essence, Thy sanctity and exaltation above the world of being and all that is therein.

O my God! Thou seest me detached from all save Thee, holding fast unto Thee and turning unto the ocean of Thy bounty, to the heaven of Thy favor, to the Daystar of Thy grace.

Lord! I bear witness that in Thy servant Thou hast reposed Thy Trust, and that is the Spirit wherewith Thou hast given life to the world.

I ask of Thee by the splendor of the Orb of Thy Revelation, mercifully to accept from him that which he hath achieved in Thy days. Grant then that he may be invested with the glory of Thy good-pleasure and adorned with Thine acceptance.

O my Lord! I myself and all created things bear witness unto Thy might, and I pray Thee not to turn away from Thyself this spirit that hath ascended unto Thee, unto Thy heavenly place, Thine exalted Paradise and Thy retreats of nearness, O Thou who art the Lord of all men!

Grant, then, O my God, that Thy servant may consort with Thy chosen ones, Thy saints and Thy Messengers in heavenly places that the pen cannot tell nor the tongue recount.

O My Lord, the poor one hath verily hastened unto the Kingdom of Thy wealth, the stranger unto his home within Thy precincts, he that is sore athirst to the heavenly river of Thy bounty. Deprive him not, O Lord, from his share of the banquet of Thy grace and from the favor of Thy bounty. Thou art in truth the Almighty, the Gracious, the All-Bountiful.

O my God, Thy Trust hath been returned unto Thee. It behooveth Thy grace and Thy bounty that have compassed Thy dominions on earth and in heaven, to vouchsafe unto Thy newly welcomed one Thy gifts and Thy bestowals, and the fruits of the tree of Thy grace! Powerful art Thou to do as Thou willest, there is none other God but Thee, the Gracious, the Most Bountiful, the Compassionate, the Bestower, the Pardoner, the Precious, the All-Knowing.

I testify, O my Lord, that Thou hast enjoined upon men to honor their guest, and he that hath ascended unto Thee hath verily reached Thee and attained Thy Presence. Deal with him then according to Thy grace and bounty! By Thy glory, I know of a certainty that Thou wilt not withhold Thyself from that which Thou hast commanded Thy servants, nor wilt Thou deprive him that hath clung to the cord of Thy bounty and hath ascended to the Dayspring of Thy wealth.

There is none other God but Thee, the One, the Single, the Powerful, the Omniscient, the Bountiful.

BAHÁ'U'LLÁH 6

I beseech Thee . . . O Thou Who art the Enlightener of the world and the Lord of the nations, at this very moment when, with the hands of hope, I have clung to the hem of the raiment of Thy mercy and Thy bounty, to forgive Thy servants who have soared in the atmosphere of Thy nearness, and set their faces towards the splendors of the light of Thy countenance, and turned unto the horizon of Thy good pleasure, and approached the ocean of Thy mercy, and all their lives long have spoken forth Thy praise, and have been inflamed with the fire of their love for Thee. Do Thou ordain for them, O Lord my God, both before and after their death, what becometh the loftiness of Thy bounty and the excellence of Thy loving-kindness.

Grant, O my Lord, that they who have ascended unto Thee may repair unto Him Who is the most exalted Companion, and abide beneath the shadow of the Tabernacle of Thy majesty and the Sanctuary of Thy glory. Sprinkle, O my Lord, upon them from the ocean of Thy forgiveness what will make them worthy to abide, so long as Thine own sovereignty endureth, within Thy most exalted kingdom and Thine all-highest dominion. Potent art Thou to do what pleaseth Thee.

BAHÁ'U'LLÁH 7

O Lord! In this Most Great Dispensation Thou dost accept the intercession of children in behalf of their parents. This is one of the special infinite bestowals of this Dispensation. Therefore, O Thou kind Lord, accept the request of this Thy servant at the threshold of Thy singleness and submerge his father in the ocean of Thy grace, because this son hath arisen to render Thee service and is exerting effort at all times in the pathway of Thy love. Verily, Thou art the Giver, the Forgiver and the Kind!

'ABDU'L-BAHÁ 8

O Thou, my God, Who guidest the seeker to the pathway that leadeth aright, Who deliverest the lost and blinded soul out of the wastes of perdition, Thou Who bestowest upon the sincere great bounties and favors, Who guardest the frightened within Thine impregnable refuge, Who answerest, from Thine all-highest horizon, the cry of those who cry out unto Thee. Praised be Thou, O my Lord! Thou hast guided the distracted out of the death of unbelief, and hast brought those who draw nigh unto Thee to the journey's goal, and hast rejoiced the assured among Thy servants by granting them their most cherished desires, and hast, from Thy Kingdom of beauty, opened before the faces of those who yearn after Thee the gates of reunion, and hast rescued them from the fires of deprivation and loss—so that they hastened unto Thee and gained Thy presence, and arrived at Thy welcoming door, and received of gifts an abundant share.

O my Lord, they thirsted, Thou didst lift to their parched lips the waters of reunion. O Tender One, Bestowing One, Thou didst calm their pain with the balm of Thy bounty and grace, and didst heal their ailments with the sovereign medicine of Thy compassion. O Lord, make firm their feet on Thy straight path, make wide for them the needle's eye, and cause them, dressed in royal robes, to walk in glory for ever and ever.

Verily, art Thou the Generous, the Ever-Giving, the Precious, the Most Bountiful. There is none other God but Thee, the Mighty, the Powerful, the Exalted, the Victorious.

'Abdu'l-Bahá 9

O God, my God! This is Thy radiant servant, Thy spiritual thrall, who hath drawn nigh unto Thee and approached Thy presence. He hath turned his face unto Thine, acknowledging Thy oneness, confessing Thy singleness, and he hath called out in Thy name among the nations, and led the people to the streaming waters of Thy mercy, O Thou Most generous Lord! To those who asked He hath given to drink from the cup of guidance that brimmeth over with the wine of Thy measureless grace.

O Lord, assist him under all conditions, cause him to learn Thy well-guarded mysteries, and shower down upon him Thy hidden pearls. Make of him a banner rippling from castle summits in the winds of Thy heavenly aid, make of him a wellspring of crystal waters.

O my forgiving Lord! Light up the hearts with the rays of a lamp that sheddeth abroad its beams, disclosing to those among Thy people whom Thou hast bounteously favored, the realities of all things.

Verily, Thou art the Mighty, the Powerful, the Protector, the Strong, the Beneficent! Verily, Thou art the Lord of all mercies!

'ABDU'L-BAHÁ 10

O my God! O Thou forgiver of sins, bestower of gifts, dispeller of afflictions!

Verily, I beseech Thee to forgive the sins of such as have abandoned the physical garment and have ascended to the spiritual world.

O my Lord! Purify them from trespasses, dispel their sorrows, and change their darkness into light. Cause them to enter the garden of happiness, cleanse them with the most pure water, and grant them to behold Thy splendors on the loftiest mount.

'ABDU'L-BAHÁ 11

O Thou forgiving Lord!

Although some souls have spent the days of their lives in ignorance, and became estranged and contumacious, yet, with one wave from the ocean of Thy forgiveness, all those encompassed by sin will be set free. Whomsoever Thou willest Thou makest a confidant, and whosoever is not the object of Thy choice is accounted a transgressor. Shouldst Thou deal with us with Thy justice, we are all naught but sinners and deserving to be shut out from Thee, but shouldst Thou uphold mercy, every sinner would be made pure and every stranger a friend. Bestow, then, Thy forgiveness and pardon, and grant Thy mercy unto all.

Thou art the Forgiver, the Lightgiver and the Omnipotent.

'Abdu'l-Bahá 12

O my God! O my God! Verily thy servant, humble before the majesty of Thy divine supremacy, lowly at the door of Thy oneness, hath believed in Thee and in Thy verses, hath testified to Thy word, hath been enkindled with the fire of Thy love, hath been immersed in the depths of the ocean of Thy knowledge, hath been attracted by Thy breezes, hath relied upon Thee, hath turned his face to Thee, hath offered his supplications to Thee, and hath been assured of Thy pardon and forgiveness. He hath abandoned this mortal life and hath flown to the kingdom of immortality, yearning for the favor of meeting Thee.

O Lord, glorify his station, shelter him under the pavilion of Thy supreme mercy, cause him to enter Thy glorious paradise, and perpetuate his existence in Thine exalted rose garden, that he may plunge into the sea of light in the world of mysteries.

Verily, Thou art the Generous, the Powerful, the Forgiver
and the Bestower.

'ABDU'L-BAHÁ 13

PRAYERS OF SOLACE
FOR THE BEREAVED

Dispel my grief by Thy bounty and Thy generosity, O God,
my God, and banish mine anguish through Thy sovereignty and Thy might. Thou seest me, O my God, with my face
set towards Thee at a time when sorrows have compassed me on
every side. I implore Thee, O Thou Who art the Lord of all being,
and overshadowest all things visible and invisible, by Thy Name
whereby Thou hast subdued the hearts and the souls of men, and
by the billows of the Ocean of Thy mercy and the splendors of
the Daystar of Thy bounty, to number me with them whom
nothing whatsoever hath deterred from setting their faces toward
Thee, O Thou Lord of all names and Maker of the heavens!

Thou beholdest, O my Lord, the things which have befallen
me in Thy days. I entreat Thee, by Him Who is the Dayspring of
Thy names and the Dawning-Place of Thine attributes, to ordain
for me what will enable me to arise to serve Thee and to extol Thy
virtues. Thou art, verily, the Almighty, the Most Powerful, Who
art wont to answer the prayers of all men!

And, finally, I beg of Thee by the light of Thy countenance
to bless my affairs, and redeem my debts, and satisfy my needs.

Thou art He to Whose power and to Whose dominion every tongue hath testified, and Whose majesty and Whose sovereignty every understanding heart hath acknowledged. No God is there but Thee, Who hearest and art ready to answer.

BAHÁ'U'LLÁH 14

O Thou Whose tests are a healing medicine to such as are nigh unto Thee, Whose sword is the ardent desire of all them that love Thee, Whose dart is the dearest wish of those hearts that yearn after Thee, Whose decree is the sole hope of them that have recognized Thy truth! I implore Thee, by Thy divine sweetness and by the splendors of the glory of Thy face, to send down upon us from Thy retreats on high that which will enable us to draw nigh unto Thee. Set, then, our feet firm, O my God, in Thy Cause, and enlighten our hearts with the effulgence of Thy knowledge, and illumine our breasts with the brightness of Thy names.

BAHÁ'U'LLÁH 15

Lauded and glorified art Thou, O my God! I entreat Thee by the sighing of Thy lovers and by the tears shed by them that long to behold Thee, not to withhold from me Thy tender mercies in Thy Day, nor to deprive me of the melodies of the Dove that extolleth Thy oneness before the light that shineth from Thy face. I am the one who is in misery, O God! Behold me cleaving fast to Thy Name, the All-Possessing. I am the one who is sure to perish; behold me clinging to Thy Name, the Imperishable. I implore Thee, therefore, by Thy Self, the Exalted, the Most High, not to abandon me unto mine own self and unto the desires of a corrupt inclination. Hold Thou my hand with the hand of Thy power, and deliver me from the depths of my fancies and idle imaginings, and cleanse me of all that is abhorrent unto Thee.

Cause me, then, to turn wholly unto Thee, to put my whole trust in Thee, to seek Thee as my Refuge, and to flee unto Thy face. Thou art, verily, He Who, through the power of His might, doeth whatsoever He desireth, and commandeth, through the potency of His will, whatsoever He chooseth. None can withstand the operation of Thy decree; none can divert the course of Thine appointment. Thou art, in truth, the Almighty, the All-Glorious, the Most Bountiful.

BAHÁ'U'LLÁH 16

Is there any Remover of difficulties save God? Say: Praised be God! He is God! All are His servants, and all abide by His bidding!

THE BÁB 17

Say: God sufficeth all things above all things, and nothing in the heavens or in the earth but God sufficeth. Verily, He is in Himself the Knower, the Sustainer, the Omnipotent.

THE BÁB 18

I adjure Thee by Thy might, O my God! Let no harm beset me in times of tests, and in moments of heedlessness guide my steps aright through Thine inspiration. Thou art God, potent art Thou to do what Thou desirest. No one can withstand Thy Will or thwart Thy Purpose.

THE BÁB 19

Thou knowest full well, O my God, that tribulations have showered upon me from all directions and that no one can dispel or transmute them except Thee. I know of a certainty, by virtue of my love for Thee, that Thou wilt never cause tribulations to befall any soul unless Thou desirest to exalt his station in Thy celestial Paradise and to buttress his heart in this earthly life with the bulwark of Thine all-compelling power, that it may not become inclined toward the vanities of this world. Indeed Thou art well aware that under all conditions I would cherish the remembrance of Thee far more than the ownership of all that is in the heavens and on the earth.

Strengthen my heart, O my God, in Thine obedience and in Thy love, and grant that I may be clear of the entire company of Thine adversaries. Verily, I swear by Thy glory that I yearn for naught besides Thyself, nor do I desire anything except Thy mercy, nor am I apprehensive of aught save Thy justice. I beg Thee to forgive me as well as those whom Thou lovest, howsoever Thou pleasest. Verily, Thou art the Almighty, the Bountiful.

Immensely exalted art Thou, O Lord of the heavens and earth, above the praise of all men, and may peace be upon Thy faithful servants and glory be unto God, the Lord of all the worlds.

THE BÁB 20

O Lord, my God and my Haven in my distress! My Shield and my Shelter in my woes! My Asylum and Refuge in time of need and in my loneliness my Companion! In my anguish my Solace, and in my solitude a loving Friend! The Remover of the pangs of my sorrows and the Pardoner of my sins!

Wholly unto Thee do I turn, fervently imploring Thee with all my heart, my mind and my tongue, to shield me from all that runs counter to Thy will in this, the cycle of Thy divine unity, and to cleanse me of all defilement that will hinder me from seeking, stainless and unsullied, the shade of the tree of Thy grace.

Have mercy, O Lord, on the feeble, make whole the sick, and quench the burning thirst.

Gladden the bosom wherein the fire of Thy love doth smolder, and set it aglow with the flame of Thy celestial love and spirit.

Robe the tabernacles of divine unity with the vesture of holiness, and set upon my head the crown of Thy favor.

Illumine my face with the radiance of the orb of Thy bounty, and graciously aid me in ministering at Thy holy threshold.

Make my heart overflow with love for Thy creatures and grant that I may become the sign of Thy mercy, the token of Thy grace, the promoter of concord amongst Thy loved ones, devoted unto Thee, uttering Thy commemoration and forgetful of self but ever mindful of what is Thine.

O God, my God! Stay not from me the gentle gales of Thy pardon and grace, and deprive me not of the wellsprings of Thine aid and favor.

'Neath the shade of Thy protecting wings let me nestle, and cast upon me the glance of Thine all-protecting eye.

Loose my tongue to laud Thy name amidst Thy people, that my voice may be raised in great assemblies and from my lips may stream the flood of Thy praise.

Thou art, in all truth, the Gracious, the Glorified, the Mighty, the Omnipotent.

'ABDU'L-BAHÁ 21

O God! Refresh and gladden my spirit. Purify my heart. Illumine my powers. I lay all my affairs in Thy hand. Thou art my Guide and my Refuge. I will no longer be sorrowful and grieved; I will be a happy and joyful being. O God! I will no longer be full of anxiety, nor will I let trouble harass me. I will not dwell on the unpleasant things of life.

O God! Thou art more friend to me than I am to myself. I dedicate myself to Thee, O Lord.

'ABDU'L-BAHÁ 22

PRAYERS FOR SPIRITUAL AWAKENING AND DEVELOPMENT

Glorified art Thou, O Lord my God! I give Thee thanks inasmuch as Thou hast called me into being in Thy days, and infused into me Thy love and Thy knowledge. I beseech Thee, by Thy name whereby the goodly pearls of Thy wisdom and Thine utterance were brought forth out of the treasuries of the hearts of such of Thy servants as are nigh unto Thee, and through which the Daystar of Thy name, the Compassionate, hath shed its radiance upon all that are in Thy heaven and on Thy earth, to supply me, by Thy grace and bounty, with Thy wondrous and hidden bounties.

These are the earliest days of my life, O my God, which Thou hast linked with Thine own days. Now that Thou hast conferred upon me so great an honor, withhold not from me the things

Thou hast ordained for Thy chosen ones.

I am, O my God, but a tiny seed which Thou hast sown in the soil of Thy love, and caused to spring forth by the hand of Thy bounty. This seed craveth, therefore, in its inmost being, for the waters of Thy mercy and the living fountain of Thy grace. Send down upon it, from the heaven of Thy loving-kindness, that which will enable it to flourish beneath Thy shadow and within the borders of Thy court. Thou art He Who watereth the hearts of all that have recognized Thee from Thy plenteous stream and the fountain of Thy living waters.

Praised be God, the Lord of the worlds.

BAHÁ'U'LLÁH 23

Praise be unto Thee, O my God! I am one of Thy servants, who hath believed on Thee and on Thy signs. Thou seest how I have set myself towards the door of Thy mercy, and turned my face in the direction of Thy loving-kindness. I beseech Thee, by Thy most excellent titles and Thy most exalted attributes, to open to my face the portals of Thy bestowals. Aid me, then, to do that which is good, O Thou Who art the Possessor of all names and attributes!

I am poor, O my Lord, and Thou art the Rich. I have set my face towards Thee, and detached myself from all but Thee. Deprive me not, I implore Thee, of the breezes of Thy tender mercy, and withhold not from me what Thou didst ordain for the chosen among Thy servants.

Remove the veil from mine eyes, O my Lord, that I may recognize what Thou hast desired for Thy creatures, and discover, in all the manifestations of Thy handiwork, the revelations of Thine almighty power. Enrapture my soul, O my Lord, with Thy most mighty signs, and draw me out of the depths of my corrupt and evil desires. Write down, then, for me the good of this world and of the world to come. Potent art Thou to do what pleaseth Thee. No God is there but Thee, the All-Glorious, Whose help is sought by all men.

I yield Thee thanks, O my Lord, that Thou hast wakened me from my sleep, and stirred me up, and created in me the desire to perceive what most of Thy servants have failed to apprehend. Make me able, therefore, O my Lord, to behold, for love of Thee and for the sake of Thy pleasure, whatsoever Thou hast desired. Thou art He to the power of Whose might and sovereignty all things testify.

There is none other God but Thee, the Almighty, the Beneficent.

Bahá'u'lláh 24

Create in me a pure heart, O my God, and renew a tranquil conscience within me, O my Hope! Through the spirit of power confirm Thou me in Thy Cause, O my Best-Beloved, and by the light of Thy glory reveal unto me Thy path, O Thou the Goal of my desire! Through the power of Thy transcendent might lift me up unto the heaven of Thy holiness, O Source of my being, and by the breezes of Thine eternity gladden me, O Thou Who art my God! Let Thine everlasting melodies breathe tranquillity on me, O my Companion, and let the riches of Thine ancient countenance deliver me from all except Thee, O my Master, and let the tidings of the revelation of Thine incorruptible Essence bring me joy, O Thou Who art the most manifest of the manifest and the most hidden of the hidden!

BAHÁ'U'LLÁH 25

From the sweet-scented streams of Thine eternity give me to drink, O my God, and of the fruits of the tree of Thy being enable me to taste, O my Hope! From the crystal springs of Thy love suffer me to quaff, O my Glory, and beneath the shadow of Thine everlasting providence let me abide, O my Light! Within the meadows of Thy nearness, before Thy presence, make me able to roam, O my Beloved, and at the right hand of the throne of Thy mercy, seat me, O my Desire! From the fragrant breezes of Thy joy let a breath pass over me, O my Goal, and into the heights of the paradise of Thy reality let me gain admission, O my Adored One! To the melodies of the dove of Thy oneness suffer me to hearken, O Resplendent One, and through the spirit of Thy power and Thy might quicken me, O my Provider! In the spirit of Thy love keep me steadfast, O my Succorer, and in the path of Thy good pleasure set firm my steps, O my Maker! Within the garden of Thine immortality, before Thy countenance, let me abide for ever, O Thou Who art merciful unto me, and upon the seat of Thy glory stablish me, O Thou Who art my Possessor! To the heaven of Thy loving-kindness lift me up, O my Quickener, and unto the Daystar of Thy guidance lead me, O Thou my Attractor! Before the revelations of Thine invisible spirit summon me to be present, O Thou Who art my Origin and my Highest Wish, and unto the essence of the fragrance of Thy beauty, which

Thou wilt manifest, cause me to return, O Thou Who art my God!
Potent art Thou to do what pleaseth Thee. Thou art, verily,
the Most Exalted, the All-Glorious, the All-Highest.

BAHÁ'U'LLÁH 26

Glorified art Thou, O Lord my God! I implore Thee by the on-
rushing winds of Thy grace, and by them Who are the Daysprings
of Thy purpose and the Dawning-Places of Thine inspiration, to
send down upon me and upon all that have sought Thy face that
which beseemeth Thy generosity and bountiful grace, and is ·
worthy of Thy bestowals and favors. Poor and desolate I am, O
my Lord! Immerse me in the ocean of Thy wealth; athirst, suffer
me to drink from the living waters of Thy loving-kindness.

I beseech Thee, by Thine own Self and by Him Whom Thou
hast appointed as the Manifestation of Thine own Being and Thy
discriminating Word unto all that are in heaven and on earth, to
gather together Thy servants beneath the shade of the Tree of
Thy gracious providence. Help them, then, to partake of its
fruits, to incline their ears to the rustling of its leaves, and to
the sweetness of the voice of the Bird that chanteth upon its
branches. Thou art, verily, the Help in Peril, the Inaccessible, the
Almighty, the Most Bountiful.

BAHÁ'U'LLÁH 27

My God, my Adored One, my King, my Desire! What tongue can
voice my thanks to Thee? I was heedless, Thou didst awaken me.
I had turned back from Thee, Thou didst graciously aid me to
turn towards Thee. I was as one dead, Thou didst quicken me

with the water of life. I was withered, Thou didst revive me with the heavenly stream of Thine utterance which hath flowed forth from the Pen of the All-Merciful.

O Divine Providence! All existence is begotten by Thy bounty; deprive it not of the waters of Thy generosity, neither do Thou withhold it from the ocean of Thy mercy. I beseech Thee to aid and assist me at all times and under all conditions, and seek from the heaven of Thy grace Thine ancient favor. Thou art, in truth, the Lord of bounty, and the Sovereign of the kingdom of eternity.

BAHÁ'U'LLÁH 28

O God, my God! I beg of Thee by the ocean of Thy healing, and by the splendors of the Daystar of Thy grace, and by Thy Name through which Thou didst subdue Thy servants, and by the pervasive power of Thy most exalted Word and the potency of Thy most august Pen, and by Thy mercy that hath preceded the creation of all who are in heaven and on earth, to purge me with the waters of Thy bounty from every affliction and disorder, and from all weakness and feebleness.

Thou seest, O my Lord, Thy suppliant waiting at the door of Thy bounty, and him who hath set his hopes on Thee clinging to the cord of Thy generosity. Deny him not, I beseech Thee, the things he seeketh from the ocean of Thy grace and the Daystar of Thy loving-kindness.

Powerful art Thou to do what pleaseth Thee. There is none other God save Thee, the Ever-Forgiving, the Most Generous.

BAHÁ'U'LLÁH 29

O my Lord! Make Thy beauty to be my food, and Thy presence my drink, and Thy pleasure my hope, and praise of Thee my action, and remembrance of Thee my companion, and the power of Thy sovereignty my succorer, and Thy habitation my home, and my dwelling-place the seat Thou hast sanctified from the limitations imposed upon them who are shut out as by a veil from Thee.

Thou art, verily, the Almighty, the All-Glorious, the Most Powerful.

BAHÁ'U'LLÁH 30

O God, Who art the Author of all Manifestations, the Source of all Sources, the Fountainhead of all Revelations, and the Wellspring of all Lights! I testify that by Thy Name the heaven of understanding hath been adorned, and the ocean of utterance hath surged, and the dispensations of Thy providence have been promulgated unto the followers of all religions.

I beseech Thee so to enrich me as to dispense with all save Thee, and be made independent of anyone except Thyself. Rain down, then, upon me out of the clouds of Thy bounty that which shall profit me in every world of Thy worlds. Assist me, then, through Thy strengthening grace, so to serve Thy Cause amidst Thy servants that I may show forth what will cause me to be remembered as long as Thine own kingdom endureth and Thy dominion will last.

This is Thy servant, O my Lord, who with his whole being hath turned unto the horizon of Thy bounty, and the ocean of Thy grace, and the heaven of Thy gifts. Do with me then as becometh Thy majesty, and Thy glory, and Thy bounteousness, and Thy grace.

Thou, in truth, art the God of strength and power, Who art meet to answer them that pray Thee. There is no God save Thee, the All-Knowing, the All-Wise.

BAHÁ'U'LLÁH 31

Magnified be Thy name, O Lord my God! Thou art He Whom all things worship and Who worshipeth no one, Who is the Lord of all things and is the vassal of none, Who knoweth all things and is known of none. Thou didst wish to make Thyself known unto men; therefore, Thou didst, through a word of Thy mouth, bring creation into being and fashion the universe. There is none other God except Thee, the Fashioner, the Creator, the Almighty, the Most Powerful.

I implore Thee, by this very word that hath shone forth above the horizon of Thy will, to enable me to drink deep of the living waters through which Thou hast vivified the hearts of Thy chosen ones and quickened the souls of them that love Thee, that I may, at all times and under all conditions, turn my face wholly towards Thee.

Thou art the God of power, of glory and bounty. No God is there beside Thee, the Supreme Ruler, the All-Glorious, the Omniscient.

BAHÁ'U'LLÁH 32

I know not, O my God, what the Fire is which Thou didst kindle in Thy land. Earth can never cloud its splendor, nor water quench its flame. All the peoples of the world are powerless to resist its force. Great is the blessedness of him that hath drawn nigh unto it, and heard its roaring.

Some, O my God, Thou didst, through Thy strengthening

grace, enable to approach it, while others Thou didst keep back by reason of what their hands have wrought in Thy days. Whoso hath hasted towards it and attained unto it hath, in his eagerness to gaze on Thy beauty, yielded his life in Thy path, and ascended unto Thee, wholly detached from aught else except Thyself.

I beseech Thee, O my Lord, by this Fire which blazeth and rageth in the world of creation, to rend asunder the veils that have hindered me from appearing before the throne of Thy majesty, and from standing at the door of Thy gate. Do Thou ordain for me, O my Lord, every good thing Thou didst send down in Thy Book, and suffer me not to be far removed from the shelter of Thy mercy.

Powerful art Thou to do what pleaseth Thee. Thou art, verily, the All-Powerful, the Most Generous.

BAHÁ'U'LLÁH 33

He is the prayer-hearing, prayer-answering God!

By Thy glory, O Beloved One, Thou giver of light to the world! The flames of separation have consumed me, and my waywardness hath melted my heart within me. I ask of Thee, by Thy Most Great Name, O Thou the Desire of the world and the Well-Beloved of mankind, to grant that the breeze of Thine inspiration may sustain my soul, that Thy wondrous voice may reach my ear, that my eyes may behold Thy signs and Thy light as revealed in the manifestations of Thy names and Thine attributes, O Thou within Whose grasp are all things!

Thou seest, O Lord my God, the tears of Thy favored ones, shed because of their separation from Thee, and the fears of Thy devoted ones in their remoteness from Thy Holy Court. By Thy power, that swayeth all things, visible and invisible! It behooveth Thy loved ones to shed tears of blood for that which hath befallen the faithful at the hands of the wicked and the oppressors on the earth. Thou beholdest, O my God, how the ungodly have compassed Thy cities and Thy realms! I ask Thee by Thy messengers and Thy chosen ones and by Him whereby the standard of Thy divine unity hath been implanted amidst Thy servants, to shield them by Thy bounty. Thou art, verily, the Gracious, the All-Bountiful.

And, again, I ask Thee by the sweet showers of Thy grace and the billows of the ocean of Thy favor, to ordain for Thy saints that which shall solace their eyes and comfort their hearts. Lord! Thou seest him that kneeleth yearning to arise and serve Thee, the dead calling for eternal life from the ocean of Thy favor and craving to soar to the heavens of Thy wealth, the stranger longing for his home of glory 'neath the canopy of Thy grace, the seeker hastening by Thy mercy to Thy door of bounty, the sinful turning to the ocean of forgiveness and pardon.

By Thy sovereignty, O Thou Who art glorified in the hearts of men! I have turned to Thee, forsaking mine own will and desire, that Thy holy will and pleasure may rule within me and direct me according to that which the pen of Thy eternal decree hath destined for me. This servant, O Lord, though helpless turneth to the Orb of Thy Power, though abased hasteneth unto the Dayspring of Glory, though needy craveth the Ocean of Thy Grace. I beseech Thee by Thy favor and bounty, cast him not away.

Thou art verily the Almighty, the Pardoner, the Compassionate.

BAHÁ'U'LLÁH 34

O my God, the God of bounty and mercy! Thou art that King by Whose commanding word the whole creation hath been called into being; and Thou art that All-Bountiful One the doings of Whose servants have never hindered Him from showing forth His grace, nor have they frustrated the revelations of His bounty.

Suffer this servant, I beseech Thee, to attain unto that which is the cause of his salvation in every world of Thy worlds. Thou art, verily, the Almighty, the Most Powerful, the All-Knowing, the All-Wise.

BAHÁ'U'LLÁH 35

Glory be unto Thee, O God. How can I make mention of Thee while Thou art sanctified from the praise of all mankind. Magnified be Thy Name, O God, Thou art the King, the Eternal Truth; Thou knowest what is in the heavens and on the earth, and unto Thee must all return. Thou hast sent down Thy divinely ordained Revelation according to a clear measure. Praised art Thou, O Lord! At Thy behest Thou dost render victorious whomsoever Thou willest, through the hosts of heaven and earth and whatsoever existeth between them. Thou art the Sovereign, the Eternal Truth, the Lord of invincible might.

Glorified art Thou, O Lord, Thou forgivest at all times the sins of such among Thy servants as implore Thy pardon. Wash away my sins and the sins of those who seek Thy forgiveness at dawn, who pray to Thee in the daytime and in the night season, who yearn after naught save God, who offer up whatsoever God hath graciously bestowed upon them, who celebrate Thy praise at morn and eventide, and who are not remiss in their duties.

THE BÁB 36

O Lord! Thou art the Remover of every anguish and the Dispeller of every affliction. Thou art He Who banisheth every sorrow and setteth free every slave, the Redeemer of every soul. O Lord! Grant deliverance through Thy mercy, and reckon me among such servants of Thine as have gained salvation.

THE BÁB 37

Do Thou ordain for me, O Lord, every good thing Thou hast created or wilt create, and shield me from whatever evil Thou abhorrest from among the things Thou hast caused or wilt cause to exist. In truth Thy knowledge embraceth all things. Praised be Thou, verily no God is there but Thee, and nothing whatsoever in the heavens or on the earth and all that is between them can ever thwart Thy Purpose. Indeed potent art Thou over all things.

Far be it from the sublimity of Thy Being, O my God, that anyone seek Thy loving-kindness or favor. Far be it from Thy transcendent glory that anyone entreat Thee for the evidences of Thy bestowals and tender mercy. Too high art Thou for any soul to beseech the revelation of Thy gracious providence and loving care, and too sanctified is Thy glory for anyone to beg of Thee the outpourings of Thy blessings and of Thy heavenly bounty and grace. Throughout Thy kingdom of heaven and earth, which is endowed with manifold bounties, Thou art immeasurably glorified above aught whereunto any identity could be ascribed.

All that I beg of Thee, O my God, is to enable me, ere my soul departeth from my body, to attain Thy good-pleasure, even were it granted to me for a moment tinier than the infinitesimal fraction of a mustard seed. For if it departeth while Thou art pleased with me, then I shall be free from every concern or anxiety; but if it abandoneth me while Thou art displeased with me, then, even had I wrought every good deed, none would be of any avail, and had I earned every honor and glory, none would serve to exalt me.

I earnestly beseech Thee then, O my God, to graciously bestow Thy good-pleasure upon me when Thou dost cause me to ascend unto Thee and make me appear before Thy holy presence, inasmuch as Thou hast, from everlasting, been the God of immense bounty unto the people of Thy realm, and the Lord of most excellent gifts to all that dwell in the exalted heaven of Thine omnipotence.

THE BÁB 38

O compassionate God! Thanks be to Thee for Thou hast awakened and made me conscious. Thou hast given me a seeing eye and favored me with a hearing ear, hast led me to Thy kingdom and guided me to Thy path. Thou hast shown me the right way and caused me to enter the ark of Deliverance. O God! Keep me steadfast and make me firm and staunch. Protect me from violent tests and preserve and shelter me in the strongly fortified fortress of Thy Covenant and Testament. Thou art the Powerful. Thou art the Seeing. Thou art the Hearing.

O Thou the Compassionate God. Bestow upon me a heart which, like unto a glass, may be illumined with the light of Thy love, and confer upon me thoughts which may change this world into a rose garden through the outpourings of heavenly grace.

Thou art the Compassionate, the Merciful. Thou art the Great Beneficent God.

'ABDU'L-BAHÁ 39

O God, my God! Fill up for me the cup of detachment from all things, and in the assembly of Thy splendors and bestowals, rejoice me with the wine of loving Thee. Free me from the assaults of passion and desire, break off from me the shackles of this nether world, draw me with rapture unto Thy supernal realm, and refresh me amongst the handmaids with the breathings of Thy holiness.

O Lord, brighten Thou my face with the lights of Thy bestowals, light Thou mine eyes with beholding the signs of Thine all-subduing might; delight my heart with the glory of Thy knowledge that encompasseth all things, gladden Thou my soul with Thy soul-reviving tidings of great joy, O Thou King of this world and the Kingdom above, O Thou Lord of dominion and might, that I may spread abroad Thy signs and tokens, and proclaim Thy Cause, and promote Thy Teachings, and serve Thy Law and exalt Thy Word.

Thou art, verily, the Powerful, the Ever-Giving, the Able, the Omnipotent.

'ABDU'L-BAHÁ 40

O Thou compassionate Lord, Thou Who art generous and able! We are servants of Thine sheltered beneath Thy providence. Cast Thy glance of favor upon us. Give light to our eyes, hearing to our ears, and understanding and love to our hearts. Render our souls joyous and happy through Thy glad tidings. O Lord! Point out to us the pathway of Thy kingdom and resuscitate all of us through the breaths of the Holy Spirit. Bestow upon us life everlasting and confer upon us never-ending honor. Unify mankind and illumine the world of humanity. May we all follow Thy pathway, long for Thy good pleasure and seek the mysteries of Thy kingdom. O God! Unite us and connect our hearts with Thine indissoluble bond. Verily, Thou art the Giver, Thou art the Kind One and Thou art the Almighty.

'ABDU'L-BAHÁ 41

O my God! O my God! Glory be unto Thee for that Thou hast confirmed me to the confession of Thy oneness, attracted me unto the word of Thy singleness, enkindled me by the fire of Thy love, and occupied me with Thy mention and the service of Thy friends and maidservants.

O Lord, help me to be meek and lowly, and strengthen me in severing myself from all things and in holding to the hem of the garment of Thy glory, so that my heart may be filled with Thy love and leave no space for love of the world and attachment to its qualities.

O God! Sanctify me from all else save Thee, purge me from the dross of sins and transgressions, and cause me to possess a spiritual heart and conscience.

Verily, Thou art merciful and, verily, Thou art the Most Generous, Whose help is sought by all men.

'ABDU'L-BAHÁ 42

O God, O Thou Who hast cast Thy splendor over the luminous realities of men, shedding upon them the resplendent lights of knowledge and guidance, and hast chosen them out of all created things for this supernal grace, and hast caused them to encompass all things, to understand their inmost essence, and to disclose their mysteries, bringing them forth out of darkness into the visible world! "He verily showeth His special mercy to whomsoever He will."[2]

O Lord, help Thou Thy loved ones to acquire knowledge and the sciences and arts, and to unravel the secrets that are treasured up in the inmost reality of all created beings. Make them to hear the hidden truths that are written and embedded in the heart of all that is. Make them to be ensigns of guidance amongst all creatures, and piercing rays of the mind shedding forth their light in this, the "first life."[3] Make them to be leaders unto Thee, guides unto Thy path, runners urging men on to Thy Kingdom.

Thou verily art the Powerful, the Protector, the Potent, the Defender, the Mighty, the Most Generous.

'ABDU'L-BAHÁ 43

O seeker of Truth! If thou desirest that God may open thine eye, thou must supplicate unto God, pray to and commune with Him at midnight, saying:

O Lord, I have turned my face unto Thy kingdom of oneness and am immersed in the sea of Thy mercy. O Lord, enlighten my sight by beholding Thy lights in this dark night, and make me happy by the wine of Thy love in this wonderful age. O Lord, make me hear Thy call, and open before my face the

---

2. Qur'án 3:67
3. Qur'án 56:62

doors of Thy heaven, so that I may see the light of Thy glory and become attracted to Thy beauty.

Verily, Thou art the Giver, the Generous, the Merciful, the Forgiving.

'Abdu'l-Bahá 44

APPENDICES

1

RESPECT FOR THE DEAD

As this physical frame is the throne of the inner temple, whatever occurs to the former is felt by the latter. In reality that which takes delight in joy or is saddened by pain is the inner temple of the body, not the body itself. Since this physical body is the throne whereon the inner temple is established, God hath ordained that the body be preserved to the extent possible, so that nothing that causeth repugnance may be experienced. The inner temple beholdeth its physical frame, which is its throne. Thus, if the latter is accorded respect, it is as if the former is the recipient. The converse is likewise true.

Therefore, it hath been ordained that the dead body should be treated with the utmost honor and respect.

THE BÁB 1

2

THE POTENTIAL FOR ETERNAL UNION IN MARRIAGE

B ahá'í marriage is the commitment of the two parties one to the other, and their mutual attachment of mind and heart. Each must, however, exercise the utmost care to become thoroughly acquainted with the character of the other, that the binding covenant between them may be a tie that will endure forever. Their purpose must be this: to become loving companions and comrades and at one with each other for time and eternity. . . .

The true marriage of Bahá'ís is this, that husband and wife should be united both physically and spiritually, that they may ever improve the spiritual life of each other, and may enjoy everlasting unity throughout all the worlds of God. This is Bahá'í marriage.

'ABDU'L-BAHÁ 2

Marriage, among the mass of the people, is a physical bond, and this union can only be temporary, since it is foredoomed to a physical separation at the close.

Among the people of Bahá, however, marriage must be a union of the body and of the spirit as well, for here both husband and wife are aglow with the same wine, both are enamored of the same matchless Face, both live and move through the same spirit, both are illumined by the same glory. This connection between them is a spiritual one, hence it is a bond that will abide forever. Likewise do they enjoy strong and lasting ties in the physical world as well, for if the marriage is based both on the spirit and the body, that union is a true one, hence it will endure. If, however, the bond is physical and nothing more, it is sure to be only temporary, and must inexorably end in separation.

When, therefore, the people of Bahá undertake to marry, the union must be a true relationship, a spiritual coming together as well as a physical one, so that throughout every phase of life, and in all the worlds of God, their union will endure; for this real oneness is a gleaming out of the love of God.

In the same way, when any souls grow to be true believers, they will attain a spiritual relationship with one another, and show forth a tenderness which is not of this world. They will, all of them, become elated from a draught of divine love, and that union of theirs, that connection, will also abide forever. Souls, that is, who will consign their own selves to oblivion, strip from themselves the defects of humankind, and unchain themselves from human bondage, will beyond any doubt be illumined with the heavenly splendors of oneness, and will all attain unto real union in the world that dieth not.

'ABDU'L-BAHÁ 3

There is no teaching in the Bahá'í Faith that *"soul mates"* exist. What is meant is that marriage should lead to a profound friendship of spirit, which will endure in the next world, where there is no sex, and no giving and taking in marriage; just the way we should establish with our parents, our children, our brothers and sisters and friends a deep spiritual bond which will be everlasting, and not merely physical bonds of human relationship.

SHOGHI EFFENDI 4

3

DEATH, FATE, AND PREDESTINATION

The decrees of the Sovereign Ordainer, as related to fate and predestination, are of two kinds. Both are to be obeyed and accepted. The one is irrevocable, the other is, as termed by men, impending. To the former all must unreservedly submit, inasmuch as it is fixed and settled. God, however, is able to alter or repeal it. As the harm that must result from such a change will be greater than if the decree had remained unaltered, all, therefore, should willingly acquiesce in what God hath willed and confidently abide by the same.

The decree that is impending, however, is such that prayer and entreaty can succeed in averting it.

BAHÁ'U'LLÁH 5

God hath . . . decreed as lawful whatsoever He hath pleased to decree, and hath, through the power of His sovereign might, forbidden whatsoever He elected to forbid. . . . Men, however, have wittingly broken His law. Is such a behavior to be attributed to God, or to their proper selves? Be fair in your judgment. Every good thing is of God, and every evil thing is from yourselves.

Will ye not comprehend? This same truth hath been revealed in all the Scriptures, if ye be of them that understand. Every act ye meditate is as clear to Him as is that act when already accomplished. There is none other God besides Him. His is all creation and its empire. All stands revealed before Him; all is recorded in His holy and hidden Tablets. This fore-knowledge of God, however, should not be regarded as having caused the actions of men, just as your own previous knowledge that a certain event is to occur, or your desire that it should happen, is not and can never be the reason for its occurrence.

BAHÁ'U'LLÁH 6

Question.—Is the predestination which is mentioned in the Holy Books a decreed thing? If so, is not the effort to avoid it useless?

Answer.—Fate is of two kinds: one is decreed, and the other is conditional or impending. The decreed fate is that which cannot change or be altered, and conditional fate is that which may occur. So, for this lamp, the decreed fate is that the oil burns and will be consumed; therefore, its eventual extinction is a decree which it is impossible to alter or to change because it is a decreed fate. In the same way, in the body of man a power of life has been created, and as soon as it is destroyed and ended, the body will certainly be decomposed, so when the oil in this lamp is burnt and finished, the lamp will undoubtedly become extinguished.

But conditional fate may be likened to this: while there is still oil, a violent wind blows on the lamp, which extinguishes it. This is a conditional fate. It is wise to avoid it, to protect oneself from it, to be cautious and circumspect. But the decreed fate, which is like the finishing of the oil in the lamp, cannot be altered, changed nor delayed. It must happen; it is inevitable that the lamp will become extinguished.

'ABDU'L-BAHÁ 7

Question.—Is man a free agent in all his actions, or is he compelled and constrained?

Answer.—This question is one of the most important and abstruse of divine problems. If God wills, another day, at the beginning of dinner, we will undertake the explanation of this subject in detail; now we will explain it briefly, in a few words, as follows.[1] Some things are subject to the free will of man, such as justice, equity, tyranny and injustice, in other words, good and evil actions; it is evident and clear that these actions are, for the most part, left to the will of man. But there are certain things to which man is forced and compelled, such as sleep, death, sickness, decline of power, injuries and misfortunes; these are not subject to the will of man, and he is not responsible for them, for he is compelled to endure them. But in the choice of good and bad actions he is free, and he commits them according to his own will.

For example, if he wishes, he can pass his time in praising God, or he can be occupied with other thoughts. He can be an enkindled light through the fire of the love of God, and a philanthropist loving the world, or he can be a hater of mankind,

---

1. From one of a series of table talks that took place in Akka between 'Abdu'l-Bahá and Laura Clifford Barney between 1904 and 1906.

and engrossed with material things. He can be just or cruel. These actions and these deeds are subject to the control of the will of man himself; consequently, he is responsible for them.

Now another question arises. Man is absolutely helpless and dependent, since might and power belong especially to God. Both exaltation and humiliation depend upon the good pleasure and the will of the Most High.

It is said in the New Testament that God is like a potter who makes "one vessel unto honour, and another unto dishonour."[2] Now the dishonored vessel has no right to find fault with the potter saying, "Why did you not make me a precious cup, which is passed from hand to hand?" The meaning of this verse is that the states of beings are different. That which is in the lowest state of existence, like the mineral, has no right to complain, saying, "O God, why have You not given me the vegetable perfections?" In the same way, the plant has no right to complain that it has been deprived of the perfections of the animal world. Also it is not befitting for the animal to complain of the want of the human perfections. No, all these things are perfect in their own degree, and they must strive after the perfections of their own degree. The inferior beings, as we have said, have neither the right to, nor the fitness for, the states of the superior perfections. No, their progress must be in their own state.

Also the inaction or the movement of man depend upon the assistance of God. If he is not aided, he is not able to do either

---

2. Rom. 9:21.

good or evil. But when the help of existence comes from the Generous Lord, he is able to do both good and evil; but if the help is cut off, he remains absolutely helpless. This is why in the Holy Books they speak of the help and assistance of God. So this condition is like that of a ship which is moved by the power of the wind or steam; if this power ceases, the ship cannot move at all. Nevertheless, the rudder of the ship turns it to either side, and the power of the steam moves it in the desired direction. If it is directed to the east, it goes to the east; or if it is directed to the west, it goes to the west. This motion does not come from the ship; no, it comes from the wind or the steam.

In the same way, in all the action or inaction of man, he receives power from the help of God; but the choice of good or evil belongs to the man himself. So if a king should appoint someone to be the governor of a city, and should grant him the power of authority, and should show him the paths of justice and injustice according to the laws—if then this governor should commit injustice, although he should act by the authority and power of the king, the latter would be absolved from injustice. But if he should act with justice, he would do it also through the authority of the king, who would be pleased and satisfied.

That is to say, though the choice of good and evil belongs to man, under all circumstances he is dependent upon the sustaining help of life, which comes from the Omnipotent. The Kingdom of God is very great, and all are captives in the grasp of His Power. The servant cannot do anything by his own will; God is powerful, omnipotent, and the Helper of all beings.

'ABDU'L-BAHÁ 8

Question.—If God has knowledge of an action which will be performed by someone, and it has been written on the Tablet of Fate, is it possible to resist it?

Answer.—The foreknowledge of a thing is not the cause of its realization; for the essential knowledge of God surrounds, in the same way, the realities of things, before as well as after their existence, and it does not become the cause of their existence. It is a perfection of God. But that which was prophesied by the inspiration of God through the tongues of the Prophets, concerning the appearance of the Promised One of the Bible, was not the cause of the manifestation of Christ.

The hidden secrets of the future were revealed to the Prophets, and They thus became acquainted with the future events which They announced. This knowledge and these prophecies were not the cause of the occurrences. For example, tonight everyone knows that after seven hours the sun will rise, but this general foreknowledge does not cause the rising and appearance of the sun.

Therefore, the knowledge of God in the realm of contingency does not produce the forms of the things. On the contrary, it is purified from the past, present and future. It is identical with the reality of the things; it is not the cause of their occurrence.

In the same way, the record and the mention of a thing in the Book does not become the cause of its existence. The Prophets, through the divine inspiration, knew what would come to pass. For instance, through the divine inspiration They knew that Christ would be martyred, and They announced it. Now, was Their knowledge and information the cause of the martyrdom of

Christ? No; this knowledge is a perfection of the Prophets and did not cause the martyrdom.

The mathematicians by astronomical calculations know that at a certain time an eclipse of the moon or the sun will occur. Surely this discovery does not cause the eclipse to take place. This is, of course, only an analogy and not an exact image.

'Abdu'l-Bahá 9

These events[3] have deeper reasons. Their object and purpose is to teach man certain lessons. We are living in a day of reliance upon material conditions. Men imagine that the great size and strength of a ship, the perfection of machinery or the skill of a navigator will ensure safety, but these disasters sometimes take place that men may know that God is the real Protector. If it be the will of God to protect man, a little ship may escape destruction, whereas the greatest and most perfectly constructed vessel with the best and most skillful navigator may not survive a danger such as was present on the ocean. The purpose is that the people of the world may turn to God, the One Protector; that human souls may rely upon His preservation and know that He is the real safety. These events happen in order that man's faith may be increased and strengthened. Therefore, although we feel sad and disheartened, we must supplicate God to turn our hearts to the Kingdom and pray for these departed souls with faith in His infinite mercy so that, although they have been deprived of this

---

3. Calamities, such as the sinking of the *Titanic*.

earthly life, they may enjoy a new existence in the supreme mansions of the Heavenly Father.

Let no one imagine that these words imply that man should not be thorough and careful in his undertakings. God has endowed man with intelligence so that he may safeguard and protect himself. Therefore, he must provide and surround himself with all that scientific skill can produce. He must be deliberate, thoughtful and thorough in his purposes, build the best ship and provide the most experienced captain; yet, withal, let him rely upon God and consider God as the one Keeper. If God protects, nothing can imperil man's safety; and if it be not His will to safeguard, no amount of preparation and precaution will avail.

'ABDU'L-BAHÁ 10

4

REINCARNATION

Thou didst write of reincarnation. A belief in reincarnation goeth far back into the ancient history of almost all peoples, and was held even by the philosophers of Greece, the Roman sages, the ancient Egyptians, and the great Assyrians. Nevertheless such superstitions and sayings are but absurdities in the sight of God.

The major argument of the reincarnationists was this, that according to the justice of God, each must receive his due: whenever a man is afflicted with some calamity, for example, this is because of some wrong he hath committed. But take a child that is still in its mother's womb, the embryo but newly formed, and that child is blind, deaf, lame, defective—what sin hath such a child committed, to deserve its afflictions? They answer that, although to outward seeming the child, still in the womb, is guilty of no sin—nevertheless he perpetrated some wrong when in his previous form, and thus he came to deserve his punishment.

These individuals, however, have overlooked the following point. If creation went forward according to only one rule, how could the all-encompassing Power make Itself felt? How could the Almighty be the One Who "doeth as He pleaseth and ordaineth as He willeth"?[4]

4. Cf. Qur'án 3:35; 2:254.

Briefly, a return is indeed referred to in the Holy Scriptures, but by this is meant the return of the qualities, conditions, effects, perfections, and inner realities of the lights which recur in every dispensation. The reference is not to specific, individual souls and identities.

It may be said, for instance, that this lamplight is last night's come back again, or that last year's rose hath returned to the garden this year. Here the reference is not to the individual reality, the fixed identity, the specialized being of that other rose, rather doth it mean that the qualities, the distinctive characteristics of that other light, that other flower, are present now, in these. Those perfections, that is, those graces and gifts of a former springtime are back again this year. We say, for example, that this fruit is the same as last year's; but we are thinking only of the delicacy, bloom and freshness, and the sweet taste of it; for it is obvious that that impregnable center of reality, that specific identity, can never return.

What peace, what ease and comfort did the Holy Ones of God ever discover during Their sojourn in this nether world, that They should continually seek to come back and live this life again? Doth not a single turn at this anguish, these afflictions, these calamities, these body blows, these dire straits, suffice, that They should wish for repeated visits to the life of this world? This cup was not so sweet that one would care to drink of it a second time.

Therefore do the lovers of the Abhá Beauty wish for no other recompense but to reach that station where they may gaze upon Him in the Realm of Glory, and they walk no other path save over desert sands of longing for those exalted heights. They seek that ease and solace which will abide forever, and those bestowals that are sanctified beyond the understanding of the worldly mind.

'ABDU'L-BAHÁ 11

Question: What is your belief about reincarnation?

Answer: The subject of reincarnation has two aspects. One is that which the Hindustani people believe, and even that is subdivided into two: reincarnation and metempsychosis. According to one belief the soul goes and then returns in certain reincarnations; therefore, they say that a sick person is sick because of actions in a previous incarnation and that this is retribution. The other school of Hinduism believes that man sometimes appears as an animal—a donkey, for instance—and that this is retribution for past acts. I am referring to the beliefs in that country, the beliefs of the schools. There is a reincarnation of the prophetic mission. Jesus Christ, speaking of John the Baptist, declared he was Elias. When John the Baptist was questioned, "Art thou Elias?" he said, "I am not." These two statements are apparently contradictory, but in reality they do not contradict. The light is one light. The light which illumined this lamp last night is illuminating it tonight. This does not mean that the identical rays of light have reappeared but the virtues of illumination. The light which revealed itself through the glass reveals itself again so that we can say the light of this evening is the light of last evening relighted. This is as regards its virtues and not as regards its former identity. This is our view of reincarnation. We believe in that which Jesus Christ and all the Prophets have believed. For example, the Báb states, "I am the return of all the Prophets." This is significant of the oneness of the prophetic virtues, the oneness of power, the oneness of bestowal, the oneness of radiation, the oneness of expression, the oneness of revelation.

'ABDU'L-BAHÁ 12

Question.—What is the truth of the question of reincarnation, which is believed by some people?

Answer.—The object of what we are about to say is to explain the reality—not to deride the beliefs of other people; it is only to explain the facts; that is all. We do not oppose anyone's ideas, nor do we approve of criticism.

Know, then, that those who believe in reincarnation are of two classes: one class does not believe in the spiritual punishments and rewards of the other world, and they suppose that man by reincarnation and return to this world gains rewards and recompenses; they consider heaven and hell to be restricted to this world and do not speak of the existence of the other world. Among these there are two further divisions. One division thinks that man sometimes returns to this world in the form of an animal in order to undergo severe punishment and that, after enduring this painful torment, he will be released from the animal world and will come again into the human world; this is called transmigration. The other division thinks that from the human world one again returns to the human world, and that by this return rewards and punishments for a former life are obtained; this is called reincarnation. Neither of these classes speak of any other world besides this one.

The second sort of believers in reincarnation affirm the existence of the other world, and they consider reincarnation the means of becoming perfect—that is, they think that man, by going from and coming again to this world, will gradually acquire perfections, until he reaches the inmost perfection. In other words, that men are composed of matter and force: matter in the beginning—that is to say, in the first cycle—is imperfect, but on coming repeatedly to this world it progresses and acquires refinement and delicacy, until it becomes like a polished mirror; and force, which is no other than spirit, is realized in it with all the perfections.

This is the presentation of the subject by those who believe in reincarnation and transmigration. We have condensed it; if we entered into the details, it would take much time. This summary is sufficient. No logical arguments and proofs of this question are brought forward; they are only suppositions and inferences from conjectures, and not conclusive arguments. Proofs must be asked for from the believers in reincarnation, and not conjectures, suppositions and imaginations.

But you have asked for arguments of the impossibility of reincarnation. This is what we must now explain. The first argument for its impossibility is that the outward is the expression of the inward; the earth is the mirror of the Kingdom; the material world corresponds to the spiritual world. Now observe that in the sensible world appearances are not repeated, for no being in any respect is identical with, nor the same as, another being. The sign of singleness is visible and apparent in all things. If all the granaries of the world were full of grain, you would not find two grains absolutely alike, the same and identical without any distinction. It is certain that there will be differences and distinctions between them. As the proof of uniqueness exists in all things, and the Oneness and Unity of God is apparent in the reality of all things, the repetition of the same appearance is absolutely impossible. Therefore, reincarnation, which is the repeated appearance of the same spirit with its former essence and condition in this same world of appearance, is impossible and unrealizable. As the repetition of the same appearance is impossible and interdicted for each of the material beings, so for spiritual beings also, a return to the same condition, whether in the arc of descent or in the arc of ascent, is interdicted and impossible, for the material corresponds to the spiritual.

Nevertheless, the return of material beings with regard to species is evident; so the trees which during former years brought forth leaves, blossoms and fruits in the coming years will bring forth exactly the same leaves, blossoms and fruits. This is called the repetition of species. If anyone makes an objection saying that the leaf, the blossom and the fruit have been decomposed, and have descended from the vegetable world to the mineral world, and again have come back from the mineral world to the vegetable world, and, therefore, there has been a repetition—the answer is that the blossom, the leaf and the fruit of last year were decomposed, and these combined elements were disintegrated and were dispersed in space, and that the particles of the leaf and fruit of last year, after decomposition, have not again become combined, and have not returned. On the contrary, by the composition of new elements, the species has returned. It is the same with the human body, which after decomposition becomes disintegrated, and the elements which composed it are dispersed. If, in like manner, this body should again return from the mineral or vegetable world, it would not have exactly the same composition of elements as the former man. Those elements have been decomposed and dispersed; they are dissipated in this vast space. Afterward, other particles of elements have been combined, and a second body has been formed; it may be that one of the particles of the former individual has entered into the composition of the succeeding individual, but these particles have not been conserved and kept, exactly and completely, without addition or diminution, so that they may be combined again, and from that composition and mingling another individual may come into existence. So it cannot be proved that this body with all its particles has returned; that the former man has become the latter; and that, consequently, there has been repetition; that the spirit also, like the body, has returned; and that after death its essence has come back to this world.

If we say that this reincarnation is for acquiring perfections so that matter may become refined and delicate, and that the light of the spirit may be manifest in it with the greatest perfection, this also is mere imagination. For, even supposing we believe in this argument, still change of nature is impossible through renewal and return. The essence of imperfection, by returning, does not become the reality of perfection; complete darkness, by returning, does not become the source of light; the essence of weakness is not transformed into power and might by returning, and an earthly nature does not become a heavenly reality. The tree of Zaqqúm,[5] no matter how frequently it may come back, will not

---

5. The infernal tree mentioned in the Qur'án.

bring forth sweet fruit, and the good tree, no matter how often it may return, will not bear a bitter fruit. Therefore, it is evident that returning and coming back to the material world does not become the cause of perfection. This theory has no proofs nor evidences; it is simply an idea. No, in reality the cause of acquiring perfections is the bounty of God.

The Theosophists believe that man on the arc of ascent[6] will return many times until he reaches the Supreme Center; in that condition matter becomes a clear mirror, the light of the spirit will shine upon it with its full power, and essential perfection will be acquired. Now, this is an established and deep theological proposition, that the material worlds are terminated at the end of the arc of descent, and that the condition of man is at the end of the arc of descent, and at the beginning of the arc of ascent, which is opposite to the Supreme Center. Also, from the beginning to the end of the arc of ascent, there are numerous spiritual degrees. The arc of descent is called beginning,[7] and that of ascent is called progress.[8] The arc of descent ends in materialities, and the arc of ascent ends in spiritualities. The point of the compass in describing a circle makes no retrograde motion, for this would be contrary to the natural movement and the divine order; otherwise, the symmetry of the circle would be spoiled.

Moreover, this material world has not such value or such excellence that man, after having escaped from this cage, will

---

6. i.e., the Circle of Existence.
7. Lit., bringing forth.
8. Lit., producing something new.

desire a second time to fall into this snare. No, through the Eternal Bounty the worth and true ability of man becomes apparent and visible by traversing the degrees of existence, and not by returning. When the shell is once opened, it will be apparent and evident whether it contains a pearl or worthless matter. When once the plant has grown it will bring forth either thorns or flowers; there is no need for it to grow up again. Besides, advancing and moving in the worlds in a direct order according to the natural law is the cause of existence, and a movement contrary to the system and law of nature is the cause of nonexistence. The return of the soul after death is contrary to the natural movement, and opposed to the divine system.

Therefore, by returning, it is absolutely impossible to obtain existence; it is as if man, after being freed from the womb, should return to it a second time. Consider what a puerile imagination this is which is implied by the belief in reincarnation and transmigration. Believers in it consider the body as a vessel in which the spirit is contained, as water is contained in a cup; this water has been taken from one cup and poured into another. This is child's play. They do not realize that the spirit is an incorporeal being, and does not enter and come forth, but is only connected with the body as the sun is with the mirror. If it were thus, and the spirit by returning to this material world could pass through the degrees and attain to essential perfection, it would be better if God prolonged the life of the spirit in the material world until it had acquired perfections and graces; it then would not be necessary for it to taste of the cup of death, or to acquire a second life.

The idea that existence is restricted to this perishable world, and the denial of the existence of divine worlds, originally proceeded from the imaginations of certain believers in reincarnation; but the divine worlds are infinite. If the divine worlds culminated in this material world, creation would be futile: nay, existence would be pure child's play. The result of these endless beings, which is the noble existence of man, would come and go for a few days in this perishable dwelling, and after receiving punishments and rewards, at last all would become perfect. The divine creation and the infinite existing beings would be perfected and completed, and then the Divinity of the Lord, and the names and qualities of God, on behalf of these spiritual beings, would, as regards their effect, result in laziness and inaction! "Glory to thy Lord, the Lord Who is sanctified from all their descriptions."[9]

Such were the limited minds of the former philosophers, like Ptolemy and the others who believed and imagined that the world, life and existence were restricted to this terrestrial globe, and that this boundless space was confined within the nine spheres of heaven, and that all were empty and void. Consider how greatly their thoughts were limited and how weak their minds. Those who believe in reincarnation think that the spiritual worlds are restricted to the worlds of human imagination. Moreover, some of them, like the Druzes and the Nusayris, think that existence is restricted to this physical world. What an ignorant supposition! For in this universe of God, which appears

---

9. Cf. Qur'án 37:180.

in the most complete perfection, beauty and grandeur, the luminous stars of the material universe are innumerable! Then we must reflect how limitless and infinite are the spiritual worlds, which are the essential foundation. "Take heed ye who are endued with discernment."[10]

But let us return to our subject. In the Divine Scriptures and Holy Books "return" is spoken of, but the ignorant have not understood the meaning, and those who believed in reincarnation have made conjectures on the subject. For what the divine Prophets meant by "return" is not the return of the essence, but that of the qualities; it is not the return of the Manifestation, but that of the perfections. In the Gospel it says that John, the son of Zacharias, is Elias. These words do not mean the return of the rational soul and personality of Elias in the body of John, but rather that the perfections and qualities of Elias were manifested and appeared in John.

A lamp shone in this room last night, and when tonight another lamp shines, we say the light of last night is again shining. Water flows from a fountain; then it ceases; and when it begins to flow a second time, we say this water is the same water flowing again; or we say this light is identical with the former light. It is the same with the spring of last year, when blossoms, flowers and sweet-scented herbs bloomed, and delicious fruits were brought forth; next year we say that those delicious fruits have come back, and those blossoms, flowers and blooms have returned and come again. This does not mean that exactly the

---

10. Qur'án 59:2.

same particles composing the flowers of last year have, after decomposition, been again combined and have then come back and returned. On the contrary, the meaning is that the delicacy, freshness, delicious perfume and wonderful color of the flowers of last year are visible and apparent in exactly the same manner in the flowers of this year. Briefly, this expression refers only to the resemblance and likeness which exist between the former and latter flowers. The "return" which is mentioned in the Divine Scriptures is this: it is fully explained by the Supreme Pen[11] in the Kitáb-i-Íqán. Refer to it, so that you may be informed of the truth of the divine mysteries.

'ABDU'L-BAHÁ 13

When thou lookest about thee with a perceptive eye, thou wilt note that on this dusty earth all humankind are suffering. Here no man is at rest as a reward for what he hath performed in former lives; nor is there anyone so blissful as seemingly to pluck the fruit of bygone anguish. And if a human life, with its spiritual being, were limited to this earthly span, then what would be the harvest of creation? Indeed, what would be the effects and the outcomes of Divinity Itself? Were such a notion true, then all created things, all contingent realities, and this whole world of being—all would be meaningless. God forbid that one should hold to such a fiction and gross error.

'ABDU'L-BAHÁ 14

---

11. Bahá'u'lláh.

5

OUR SPIRITUAL AND MATERIAL CONNECTION WITH THE UNIVERSE

Question.—Have the stars of the heavens any influence upon the human soul, or have they not?

Answer.—Some of the celestial stars have a clear and apparent material effect upon the terrestrial globe and the earthly beings, which needs no explanation. Consider the sun, which through the aid and the providence of God develops the earth and all earthly beings. Without the light and heat of the sun, all the earthly creatures would be entirely nonexistent.

With regard to the spiritual influence of stars, though this influence of stars in the human world may appear strange, still, if you reflect deeply upon this subject, you will not be so much surprised at it. My meaning is not, however, that the decrees which the astrologers of former times inferred from the movements of the stars corresponded to occurrences; for the decrees of those former astrologers were forms of imagination which were originated by Egyptian, Assyrian and Chaldean priests; nay, rather, they were due to the fancies of Hindus, to the myths of the Greeks, Romans and other star worshipers. But I mean that this limitless universe is like the human body, all the members of which are connected and linked with one another with the greatest strength. How much the organs, the members and the parts of the body of man are intermingled and connected for mutual aid and help, and how much they influence one another! In the same way, the parts of this infinite universe have their members and elements connected with one another, and influence one another spiritually and materially.

For example, the eye sees, and all the body is affected; the ear hears, and all the members of the body are moved. Of this there is no doubt; and the universe is like a living person. Moreover, the connection which exists between the members of beings must necessarily have an effect and impression, whether it be material or spiritual.

For those who deny spiritual influence upon material things we mention this brief example: wonderful sounds and tones, melodies and charming voices, are accidents which affect the air—for sound is the term for vibrations of the air—and by these vibrations the nerves of the tympanum of the ear are affected, and hearing results. Now reflect that the vibration of the air, which is an accident of no importance, attracts and exhilarates the spirit of man and has great effect upon him: it makes him weep or laugh; perhaps it will influence him to such a degree that he will throw himself into danger. Therefore, see the connection which exists between the spirit of man and the atmospheric vibration, so that the movement of the air becomes the cause of transporting him from one state to another, and of entirely overpowering him; it will deprive him of patience and tranquillity. Consider how strange this is, for nothing comes forth from the singer which enters into the listener; nevertheless, a great spiritual effect is produced. Therefore, surely so great a connection between beings must have spiritual effect and influence.

It has been mentioned that the members and parts of man affect and influence one another. For example, the eye sees; the heart is affected. The ear hears; and the spirit is influenced. The heart is at rest; the thoughts become serene, and for all the members of man's body a pleasant condition is realized. What a connection and what an agreement is this! Since this connection, this spiritual effect and this influence, exists between the members of the body of man, who is only one of many finite beings, certainly between these universal and infinite beings there will also be a spiritual and material connection. Although by existing rules and actual science these connections cannot be discovered, nevertheless, their existence between all beings is certain and absolute.

To conclude: the beings, whether great or small, are connected with one another by the perfect wisdom of God, and affect and influence one another. If it were not so, in the universal system and the general arrangement of existence, there would be disorder and imperfection. But as beings are connected one with another with the greatest strength, they are in order in their places and perfect.

This subject is worthy of examination. 'ABDU'L-BAHÁ 15

REFERENCES

REFERENCES

Abbreviations Used

Note: References to *The Hidden Words* are keyed to the numbers of individual Hidden Words rather than to page numbers. References to *Tablets of the Divine Plan* are keyed to the 1993 pocket-size edition in which tablets and paragraphs are numbered (for example, "TDP 5:6" refers to tablet number 5, paragraph 6).

ABL   *'Abdu'l-Bahá in London: Addresses and Notes of Conversations,* repr. 1982

BP   *Bahá'í Prayers: A Selection of Prayers Revealed by Bahá'u'lláh, the Báb, and 'Abdu'l-Bahá,* new ed., 1991

BNE   *Bahá'u'lláh and the New Era: An Introduction to the Bahá'í Faith,* repr. 1993

BPP   *The Bahá'í Peace Program: From the Writings of 'Abdu'l-Bahá,* 1930

ESW   *Epistle to the Son of the Wolf,* pocket-size ed., repr. 1993

GWB   *Gleanings from the Writings of Bahá'u'lláh,* pocket-size ed., repr. 1990

HWA   *The Hidden Words* (Arabic), repr. 1990

HWP   *The Hidden Words* (Persian), repr. 1990

KA   *The Kitáb-i-Aqdas: The Most Holy Book,* pocket-size ed., 1993

KI   *The Kitáb-i-Íqán: The Book of Certitude,* pocket-size ed., repr. 1993

NBR   *National Bahá'í Review,* no. 92 (Sept. 1975 [B.E. 132]): p. 6

PT   *Paris Talks: Addresses Given by 'Abdu'l-Bahá in Paris in 1911,* 1969

PM   *Prayers and Meditations,* repr. 1987

PUP   *The Promulgation of Universal Peace: Talks Delivered by 'Abdu'l-Bahá during His Visit to the United States and Canada in 1912,* repr. 1991

SDC   *The Secret of Divine Civilization,* pocket-size ed., repr. 1994

SWAB   *Selections from the Writings of 'Abdu'l-Bahá,* lightweight ed., repr. 1982

SWB   *Selections from the Writings of the Báb,* lightweight ed., repr. 1982
SVFV   *The Seven Valleys and The Four Valleys,* new ed., 1991
SAQ   *Some Answered Questions,* pocket-size ed., repr. 1994
TA   *Tablets of Abdul-Baha Abbas,* vol. 3, 1916
TB   *Tablets of Bahá'u'lláh Revealed after the Kitáb-i-Aqdas,* pocket-size ed., repr. 1992
TDP   *Tablets of the Divine Plan: Revealed by 'Abdu'l-Bahá to the North American Bahá'ís,* new ed., 1993

1

DEATH: A TRANSITION TO LIFE

Returning to God

1	GWB	247
2	SWB	162
3	SWB	157
4	SWB	161
5	SWB	163
6	PUP	291

The Real World

7	GWB	329
8	SWAB	177–78
9	SWAB	220–21
10	SWAB	204
11	TDP	11:12

The Continuity of Existence

12	BPP	37
13	PUP	87–89
14	PT	90–94

Understanding Death as a Transition to Eternal Life

15	ABL	95–96
16	SWAB	200–01
17	SWAB	197
18	SWAB	199–200

19	SWAB	201
20	SAQ	240
21	SWAB	64–65
22	PUP	47–48

Meditations on the Transition to Life

23	HWA	14
24	HWA	32
25	HWA	33

2

EARTHBOUND: THE SEDUCTION OF HUMAN PLEASURES, OPPORTUNITIES FOR ATTAINING TRUE HAPPINESS

The Illusion of Earthly Life

1	GWB	261
2	TB	265-66
3	ESW	56
4	GWB	328-29
5	GWB	276
6	SWAB	186
7	TB	266-67

The Life of the Spirit Versus Material Life

8	KI	120-21
9	SAQ	241-42
10	SAQ	242-43
11	SWAB	192
12	SWAB	204-05
13	TAB	3:549
14	PUP	7
15	SWAB	191

Attaining True Paradise

16	TB	118
17	GWB	70-71
18	TB	189
19	KI	118
20	GWB	143
21	SWB	145
22	SWB	88-89
23	SWB	77

24	SWB	79
25	SWB	98–99
26	SAQ	223–25
27	GWB	345–46

Bringing Yourself to Account

28	GWB	236
29	KA	¶148
30	GWB	307–08

Meditations on the Seduction of Human Pleasures, Opportunities for Attaining True Happiness

31	HWP	75
32	HWP	40
33	HWP	37
34	HWA	63

3

THE DAILY STRUGGLE: FREEING THE SOUL'S POTENTIAL

The Soul—A Sign of God

1	GWB	158–59
2	GWB	160–61
3	SAQ	151–52

Recognizing Your Inner Reality

4	GWB	65
5	GWB	77–78
6	SAQ	235–37
7	PT	25
8	PT	17
9	PUP	464–65
10	PT	85
11	SDC	19

Understanding the Human Soul and Spirit

12	GWB	161–62
13	GWB	164–65
14	SAQ	208–09
15	SAQ	227–29
16	PT	86–87
17	PT	96–99

Developing Your Soul

18	GWB	149
19	SWAB	190
20	PUP	225–26
21	PUP	226–27
22	PUP	451–52

23	PUP	90–91
24	PUP	147–49
25	PUP	294–96
26	PT	178–79
27	SWAB	185

Meditations on Freeing the Soul's Potential

28	HWA	3
29	HWA	12
30	HWA	11
31	HWA	4
32	HWA	10
33	HWA	13
34	HWA	1

4

ETERNITY: LIFE BEYOND THIS LIFE

The Worlds of God

1	GWB	151–53
2	SVFV	32–33
3	GWB	157–58

The Nature of the World Beyond

4	GWB	157
5	PUP	304–305
6	SAQ	241–42
7	SWAB	193–94
8	SWAB	202

| 9 | NBR | 6 |
| 10 | NBR | 6 |

The Soul after Death

11	GWB	157
12	GWB	155–56
13	GWB	161
14	GWB	156–57
15	GWB	153–55
16	SWAB	194
17	SAQ	239–40
18	PT	64–67
19	SAQ	233–34

20	PT	88–90
21	SAQ	240
22	NBR	6

Meditations on Life beyond This Life

23	HWA	64
24	HWA	6
25	HWA	7
26	HWP	44
27	HWP	41
28	HWA	61

5

THIS LIFE AND THE NEXT:
DISCOVERIES, ASSOCIATION, AND COMMUNICATION

Spiritual Discoveries in This World and the Next

1	GWB	194
2	SWAB	169–70
3	SAQ	252–53
4	SWAB	170–71
5	SWAB	177

Association and Communication in This Life and the Next

6	GWB	169–71
7	BNE	190
8	PT	179
9	BNE	193
10	NBR	6

Interceding for Those in the Next World

11	SAQ	231–32
12	ABL	96

Meditations on Discoveries, Association, and Communication

13	HWP	70
14	HWP	21
15	HWP	6
16	HWP	35
17	HWP	39

6

PRAYERS AND MEDITATIONS FOR SPIRITUAL PROGRESS

Intercessions for the Departed

1	BP	40–41
2	BP	87–88
3	BP	129–30
4	BP	146
5	BP	41–42
6	BP	43–45
7	PM	278–79
8	BP	65
9	BP	167–68
10	BP	154–55
11	BP	45–46
12	BP	47
13	SWAB	196–97

Prayers of Solace for the Bereaved

14	BP	26–27
15	BP	191

16	BP	27–28
17	BP	28
18	BP	29
19	BP	29
20	BP	194–95
21	BP	30–31
22	BP	152

Prayers for Spiritual Awakening and Development

Bahá'u'lláh

23	BP	149–50
24	BP	53–55
25	BP	142–43
26	BP	141–42
27	BP	109–10
28	BP	19–20
29	BP	86

30	BP	144–45
31	BP	173–74
32	BP	122–23
33	BP	52–53
34	BP	147–49
35	BP	146

The Báb

36	BP	81–82
37	BP	29
38	SWB	187–88

'Abdu'l-Bahá

39	BP	71–72
40	BP	58–59
41	BP	100
42	BP	152–53
43	BP	103
44	BP	61–62

APPENDICES

1 Respect for the Dead

1   SWB   95

2 The Potential for Eternal Union in Marriage

2   SWAB   118
3   SWAB   117–18
4   NBR   6

3 Death, Fate, and Predestination

5   GWB   133
6   GWB   149–50
7   SAQ   244
8   SAQ   248–50
9   SAQ   138–39
10 PUP   48

4 Reincarnation

11 SWAB 183–84
12 PUP   167–68
13 SAQ   282–89
14 SWAB 184–85

5 Our Spiritual and Material Connection with the Universe

15 SAQ   245–47

65390

DATE DUE

3/17/02			